THROUGH THE EYES OF A SEAF
A COLLECTION OF EVENTS EXPER
SHORT STORIES
BY
TERRENCE J CADET

1

Where lies the land to which ship goes?
Far,far ahead,is all her semen know.
And where the land he travels from?
Away,far far behind,is all they can say.

Arthur Hugh Clough 1819-1861

Sketches artist Terrence J Cadet

I could only imagine when as a boy sat reading such novels as Treasure Island
and stories of those navigators in my hide away,then being taken,standing in the
Great Painted Galleries at Grenwich,
That one day I would also voyage to all those bewitching named islands and places.
Meeting people of all race and tongue,to listen and learn much of the many cultures
and their customs.
Many, my privilege to call many, friends.
Life at sea, is not everyone's cup of tea,,many stay a short time,other hear the call of
the sea and it becomes their life.
Much has change since those days of press ganging to man those ships that wrote
much of our maritime history

At an early age, my introduction, to life at sea was age seven. In a wooden whaler
passing under that impressive figure head of a turbaned native as it looked down at a
boat full of wide eyed boys, then walking up the gangway of that wooden Man of War
Foudroyant, anchored mid river in Portsmouth harbour. To sleep in canvas hammocks,
below deck where once those mighty cannon once roared in battle.
I was to learn much throughout my summer holiday,knots and splicing,rowing and
sailing . To visit the mighty battleship HMS Vanguard that was moored across the way.
For to a boy just seven years old from a Children's Home,to be taken to a village steam
train station in the heart of the Buckinghamshire countryside, handed to a train guard,
alone, with nothing but a letter stuffed in his pocket. then to travel to
Marlybourne,London. Where the train guard handed me to a group of Royal Navy
sailors who would look after me and get me to Portsmouth Harbour and my destination.
As I sat waiting while the sailors drank in the station bar then took me on to
Waterloo,where again I was ask to sit and wait and not move, while they again went to
the Railway Station Bar.
Then finally on another train where in the carriage they played cards on a suitcase used
as a table,smoked and drank. They were a cheerful bunch of lads and looked after me
during their care ,until arriving at my destination where they handed me over to a Navel
Officer, who I still recall him saying and pointing "Down those well worn stone steps
lad, where once Lord Nelson, himself walked down to go board the Victory"..
Guess that wouldn't happen these days, a young kid on his own to be handed to
strangers. But,it was the start of a life long adventure.

Then years later in 58,went to T.S Warfleet,where they taught Signals,Morse,
semaphore and flags. sailing and again rowing whalers,which we would row down the
Hamble River from Botley to a large motor boat the 'Western Skye', which was
anchored off Warsash. where we learnt the compass and steering by quarter points
only.
I was to go in to the Royal Navy,but I choose the Merchant instead, And not a days
regret.

A life at sea,is unlike any ashore. Every single day brings something new and refreshing- those first experiences can never be repeated.
The marine life one is so fortunate to see in their own environment and mine to share, Nowhere else can one sit with a mug of tea,in silence,and watch some amazing sunrises and sunset unhindered and watch as if in slow motion before ones vision those fiery red and orange skies change as if by the hand of an invisible artist's brushes upon a giant canvas. Reds ,oranges slowly turn to pastel colours of greys pinks greys and blues amid a plum of roseate and primrose tinted apricot clouds mirrored in the sea.
Sunrise,can be as breathtaking waiting and watching for the unfolding harmonious symphony in the peculiar impressiveness when brought upon one's vision.
 And as darkness falls and one stands on the bridge wing looking up at the clear cloudless skies with billions of stars twinkle and reflect like diamonds dancing upon the ocean-then a blue whale with calf break the surface ,blow spouts and dive showing off their massive tail flunks.

  Have always thought such experiences were a privilege to witness.
 I was once asked,"How can someone spend their life's floating on an endless ocean,day after day,it must be so boring.... Don't you miss a normal life?"
"It certainly isn't boring or empty my friend" I replied.
"Many people see such programs as Blue Planet, and are in awe at what they see".
 But to watch three thousand Pacific Spinner Dolphins, adult and juveniles heading towards you. Exploding out the ocean spinning in mid air with the reflection of a rainbow of colour from the setting sun on their bodies before splashing back down into the churning ocean that is virtuously alive".

"Mother Nature, can be a wonder,but she can also make many a man pray.
Seamen have a great respect and rapport with Mother Nature It has taken many a life over the centuries.
"Imagine waking stepping out on deck,to find every centimetre of the ships superstructure covered in things such as Ladybirds,tiger moths or small birds migrating and using the ship as a service station."No the oceans and seas are not empty". There is a freedom out there, no smog, the air is clear and clean,there is no overcrowding and bustling.
Its when a man who has spent his whole life with the motion beneath his feet steps on Terra Firma he can relate to that of a beached whale and finds it hard to adjust.
The sea has a strong pull for its own and many never really adjust.
A life at sea is unlike any ashore and I count myself among my peers and fellow seafarer.
Of whom all have share experiences and have their own stories be they Officer or Rating. These are a few of mine.

CONTENT

GHOST ON BOARD

Believe it or not.
It all kicked off during the 0000-0400 watch,on the bridge were the Second Officer, Able Seaman and a young deck boy. The ship was on course,steaming through the Newfoundland Banks.
Outside on the starboard bridge wing the Able seaman faced winters North Atlantic

bone chilling wind,sea was choppy and a few small ice-berg had been sighted and reported.

Two hours and twenty minutes into the watch, in the darkness of the wheel-house the Second Officer,was correcting his chart entering the ships position.

Once done ,he call for Paul the deck Boy, to put the kettle on for a brew.

Behind the chartroom was a small annex where such things as charts, light correction volume etc. were kept as well as the the kettle and complements for brewing.

The lad upon filling the kettle went back to the room as he drew back the curtain he stopped suddenly and when the Officer saw him just standing as if frozen to the spot asked.

"What is it lad?"

Paul never uttered a word his face was ashen as if he had seen a ghost.

Again the Second, asked "Well boy? speak up ,what's the problem?"

"Sir,in there...." his words faltered as he spoke.

What,spit it out! Can't you see I am busy?"

Paul pointed to the drawn curtain. "Sir ,there is an old man in there Sir"

"What's all this nonsense boy? Have you made the tea or not?

"The man sir he is just standing looking at a chart. sir."

Now a little annoyed at the lad,pushed by ,pulling back the curtain,entered then came out. "I am not amused boy, i far more important things to do ,than fall for your pointless sense of humour!Now get the tea made,damn you!"

Paul never moved an inch. the Officer turned to see the boy frozen and fixed to the spot.

"Are you going to make the tea or just stand there?"

"Okay that's it, I will report this to the Chief Officer, in the morning,now remove yourself from the bridge"

The Able seamen heard the raised voice and came in to the wheelhouse.

"Is there some problem here Second?"

"damn the boy ,he refuses to make the brew ,said he saw someone and won't go in there,so have sent him below and told him I will be reporting him".

With the watch over ,the seaman ,caught up with Paul and asked him to explain what went on.

He listened as Paul explained still shaken by the experience

" Well I went to make the tea as normal as requested, but as I walked in, swear I saw what looked like a figure you know as if he was a figment of my imagination ,but I saw him, old man, grey white hair and beard cap with braid and wearing a heavy black greatcoat ,leaning over the out laid charts on the desktop" he took a deep breath. "I swear its not a hoax"

As the Able Seaman, listened to the boy,he felt like someone had just walked over his grave

Following midday watch, Paul was in front of the Captain ,Chief Officer on the bridge and asked to explain what had gone on.

he repeated the incident and a note was made and entered as a phenomenon.

Upon the completion of the voyage,Paul signed off and never returned to sea.

Then during a voyage some ten years later,on a night not unlike that night in 1970,
the same ship steamed through the iced waters of the Newfoundland Banks.
Ships clock read 0220hrs.
The Navigator, needed a fresh chart and as he pulled back the curtain to enter the room
he to saw a burly short figure dress in a heavy coat with braid white hair and well
trimmed beard ,both hand placed firmly on the desktop as he was reading the chart.
In shock the navigator stepped backward and bumped in to someone standing behind
him and almost jumped a inch off his feet as he heard a voice behind him in the dark.
"Looks like you have seen a ghost Mr Stewart?"
"Aye,that I have Sir,I think?"
"Come man stand aside",as the Captain,pull aside the heavy curtain,looked in saw
nothing.
"Eyes playing tricks Mr Stewart,I think sir?

Then,suddenly the Captain turned with a strange, thoughtful look on his face as if he
was trying to remember something.
In a quiet voice said "Do we still have those old log books?"
"I do think we do Sir"
"Then find me the log for 1970 April"
Some time passed, he returned handing the log to the Captain ,who was still in his
dressing robe and slippers
Quickly flipping the pages ,stopped ran his finger down the page . Then stopped!
"Yes,yes here it is, Mr Mate,What is the time right now?"
"0234"
"And ships position?"
Reading off the SATNAV
"Oh my! now that is more than a coincident Mr Stewart, same date ,time and position"
"Listen to this entry for an incident that occurred to which I was also in command that
evening"
He read the entry, relating to an observation which recorded what occurred. at the time
on the 14th April witnessed by a young deck boy at the time believed to be a
folly,which no one believed. Both accounts were identical.
At the time and position, the last signal received from the ill fated S.S Titanic upon
being struck by the iceberg.
The Captain closed the log book turned and stated" I can only state gentlemen,
I am not one to believe in ghosts, but evidence here and witnessed, it could be no other
than Captain Smith,Master of the ill fated Titanic""
"Think I need a cuppa" Captain said.
"To be more than honest Captain I could do with something a little stronger.
"Indeed Mr Stewart! Both, walked out to the bridge wing, saying nothing just looked
over the dodger at the small berg floating by. then turning to the Able seamen said
"Keep those eyes peeled lad?"
Aye aye Captain

Homeward Bound

KERMIT SAVES THE DAY

There was or had been a long tradition on British Merchant ships at Christmas to
hoist up a small tree up its foremast and slap on a few coloured lights.
But in these modern days not many ships do. Maybe that may be due to there are
not to many ship flying the Red Duster these days,Plus to be honest not to many British
seamen which for an island that has a long history is shameful.

But this a story when times were different.

There were many liners plying back and forth across the North Atlantic,flying their national flags with pride.

The voyage from Southampton had been foul high seas and windy with rain,but we deck seamen really didn't mind we were out on deck in all weather.

While passengers layered in heavy jumpers and top coats even gloves,strolled around the Boat Deck for their morning or evening constitutional,many spending the day drape in heavy blankets stretched out on deck loungers braving the cold and being served hot drinks by smartly dressed long time served deck stewards from their small deck pantries.

The morning of our arrival at Ambrose Light,where we boarded our |American ships pilot, who would see the ship safely up under the Verrazano Bridge,some span of 4,260 feet,then up the Hudson River to our berth.

There was always a grand view of the Manhattan Skyline, and Statue of Liberty and the shoreline of New Jersey in the early morning and the smell of roasting coffee from the large Maxwell House Coffee factory that drifted on the breeze as one slipped by.

Staten Island and Circle Line ferries criss cross the river as Moran tugs secure their towing lines to assist our docking.

Once alongside and gangways in place passengers and baggage are landed as well as any cargo,the morning is filled with much activity. around 1330 the Christmas trees were slung aboard,the large for pubic rooms and stair wells and few for crew and one for the ships mast.

Which we carried up to the Monkey Island, above the ships bridge.

(Monkey Island arrive from the terminology where gunpowder was kept and collected by young lads -powder monkeys during British Navel battles of the 19th Century)

We had flipped a coin and I got to go aloft in a bosun's chair,so wrapped up warm as a chilling wind blew down river and snow began to fall.

Once high above the deck at least I had a good view of the Big Apple while swinging around(No such thing as safety harness, hard hat back then ...just old school)

Below long -shore men ,were busy loading stores and goods.

Under the overpass Yellow and Chequered cabs came and went picking up and dropping off people.

Meanwhile a pull on my gantline was to hoist up first a galvanized bucket with fixtures then another to hoist the Christmas tree..

Snow fell harder and wind didn't help fixing the tree to the truck,but finally it was secure. Next were the fairy lights and cable when fixed the only remaining decoration was the Star of David to top it off.

But..while hoisting it up in the bucket it snagged and tipped the bucket .. and from up high all I heard was the shattering when it hit the metal deck.

Sat up the mast I wondered what we were going to do to top off the tree ... waiting until felt a pull on my line and hoisted up the replacement.

To my surprise it certainly was a Star. But I secured the 'Christmas Fairy' to the top.

I thought it looked great.

Once back on deck ,the lads were having a laugh all agreed it was different.

We were heading for a Caribbean cruise .

When we got ready to sail that evening a tannoy broke the night inviting passengers to come see the light being turned on. The count down began Three, Two, One. There were cameras flashes going off amid the clapping and cheering.

   It was the CPO Coxswain ,Bill who filled us in, over a pint in the Pig & Whistle what the reaction on the bridge was. He said the moment the light came on he heard the Captain ask "Where's my Star of David?

   He reached for his binoculars and looked up. then was then heard to say "What the bloody hell is that on top my tree certainly doesn't look like a star "Handing the Chief Officer his glasses

"Now tell me that isn't a damn frog waving its arms and legs up there?

The mate turned "Yes Sir, I do believe it is a frog!!!!.

Bill said "I do believe I heard the Captain laugh"

Then said "Well its up there now and can bloody well stay there".

   And so it did the whole Festive Season holidays. It was on the East bound voyage home half way across the North Atlantic after high winds one morning Kermit the Frog was gone.

"But hey, frogs are good swimmers ...Right?"

STEINBECK GOES RASPBERY

1965

A day that began like the past two week ,sun hot beating down -the kind that has
one dripping in perspiration in less than a few minutes of stepping on deck for another
day of chipping, descaling,wire brushing loose paint and rust off derricks,hatch
combing,winches and bollards.
 Six of us Deckies, all brown as roasted coffee beans plying port of South America and
Central Americas and a few other unheard of places,wearing nothing but cut off's,flip
flops, and a smile.

Then there was 'Steinbeck' the ships tortoise, who turned out that morning
strolling across the stained canvas hatch tarpaulin at his normal speed which varied
from 'dead slow' and 'finished with engines'. Spoon's the old Bosun, named because of
his talent when having one to many would turn up playing his spoons on his bony
knees,had mentioned Steinbeck had been aboard for almost six years
Some seaman brought it onboard and when he signed off the tortoise remained.
recall asking Spoon's "How come Steinbeck Bosun?"
 he said "You may have noticed the number of dog eared paperback books floating
around,well someone name the tortoise and it seems to have stuck"
It was right everywhere one went a Steinbeck paper back, even rolled up behind the
bog house water pipe. Guess if one is in their long enough one could get through a
chapter or two.
. I was reading "Travels With Charley".

Any way's we were hammerer and chipped away till smoko, then back out till noon.
wire brushing all the bare metal making ready for priming with red lead.
Now there was a "Golden Rule" at sea,No noise,shouting or music between the hours
of 1200hrs -1400hrs as watch keepers below.
 Have to say, one only broke that rule once,it wasn't uncommon to witness a watch
keeper come screaming out of their cabin wearing nothing but a pair of skiddies even
naked and plant one on the offender before returning to their pit to get in a few more
hours before picking up their watch.
Can't recall to many lads doing it a second time! But hey,I am making a reference to
the good old days when things were much different,unlike these modern days where,
that rule has gone out the porthole, no consideration for others.
Back then it was work hard and learnt to duck.

With lunch over it was back out in the scorching sun,the metal plated deck was hot enough to fry an egg even melt ones flip flops.

Down in the forward paint/lamp stores as hot as a ships cook 's oven we got our paint,back on deck gave everything a couple of coats of red led it was known to add some varnish to the red lead certainly held back any rust longer.

Now Steinbeck, hadn't moved far, as he found shelter in the shadow of the fore mast that wandered across the canvas hatch tarpaulin.

At 1500,we stopped for afternoon smoko,, that ranged from water,tea juice or a few good slugs of vodka. some of us would just find some shade and chill for half hour.

Our cabins were were hotter than hell hotter than outside at times, certainly no air conditioning. Just a old metal wind chute stuck in the porthole to catch the slightest breeze with maybe a wire gauze to keep out any unwanted creepy crawlies .

Never close in fine or foul weather. the guy in the top bunk closest to the porthole would lay his oilskins jacket over himself to avoid getting to wet.

Damn do miss those days!

So there we were happy as sand boys painting away when Geordie, ,Asked if anyone had seen Steinbeck.

A quick recce then someone shouted "Hey lads found the dopey bugger, looks like he nose dived in to someone's paint pot".

The chief Mate just happen to walk out on to the bridge wing and saw us in a huddle shouted down

"What's going on down there?"

Holding up Steinbeck dripping in red lead like a giant raspberry.

"Its Steinbeck, Chief ,Think he got to hot and dived in to a paint pot to cool off soon have him cleaned up"

So a couple of use remove most of the paint,a ragged down with some turpentine then use some light soapy water finishing off with fish oil,on it shell,lucky enough his head hadn't been touched and was free from any paint which would have been disastrous.

Steinbeck,came up pretty good,but for some months stayed a lovely shade of fading raspberry which he was most visible .

And also to the ships cat that was often seen sat looking at Steinbeck with a strange expression. But were the best of friends.

San Bento Salvador Brazil

The palm tree will grow
Coral shall spread
But man will cease.

Bora Bora sailing for Tahiti

Imagine a place where the landscape is completely undisturbed,where wildlife has no fear of man,Where humans can walk where no other has trodden before.

Imagine a place so beautiful where by simply turning ones head can take you breath away....

COWBOYS AND ASTRONAUTS
1966

It all began in Tampa Florida, on a really barmy day in 66.Ashore in a bar known as "Seven Seas".a haunt frequented by the seafarers fraternity while in port. A United Nations of lads having a good time and far to much to drink.

Now among our number were two Welsh lads,good friends and joined at the hip so to speak.

Richie ,was one of us deckies, Michael, was a greaser/wiper and both were on a bender that afternoon.

The ship had been in port three days unloading its cargo. In two hours we would be sailing for Mobile,Alabama.

It was a fair walk back, so we drank up,collared the two Welsh lads.

but all the way back they disappeared into every bar and we had to drag them out.

finally reaching the First and Last Bar a few hundred feet from the dock ate to which they just had to stop for another drink.

So we left them to make their way back under their own steam. Hopefully before the ship sailed.

The S.S Samala, was a old counter -stern vessel with rivet plated hull, bow was straight up and down a woodbine funnel and decks covered in canvas awnings.

She had seen better days, but a good ship and a good bunch of lads,food was decent.

Later we turned to, secure and batten down the hatches and house the derricks.

Half hour before sailing the Mate came and asked if the two Welshman had returned "No Chief no sign""Well they better get their asses on board before we let go".

He was a happy bunny as he spud round and went up the the companion ladder to the bridge to let the Captain know.

Stations fore and aft were called and we signalled up the moorings.

Then we heard the singing, then Richie and Michael appeared from behind the warehouse arm in arm it was hard to see who was holding who up as the staggered back. Doing the old one forward ,two steps back dance.

Even the long shore men standing by to let go the back spring and head rope were having a good old laugh. And we on stations were cracking up.

The skipper shouted to get a jump ladder over the side but not a bright idea.

Couldn't see those two scaling that in their state,it was an accident waiting to happen.

Then what happened next was the ball breaker.

Richie, shouted up to the bridge as the Skipper looked down. heard them say.

"We, me my mate here don't wish to continue working on your rust bucket,

"So me and my mate here, have decided to become cowboys okay!"

Believe me that remark even had the ships pilot cracking up as well as us lads and long shore men..

That was the last straw the Captain ,threw his arms in the air in utter frustration at the two crew members foolishness an gave the order to let go all lines

As the ship drifted off the quay and attached a tugs line we watched the Welsh lads heading back to the First and Last outside the dock gate for refuelling.

Four days sailing saw us arrive off Dauphin Island,to pick up a ships pilot to navigate the Mobile River to our berth.
Even before we came alongside the berth ,we saw our two crew members handcuffed to two cops.
 Once moored as the pair mounted the gangway we gave them a cheer.
We heard later the immigration had picked them up,and had been thrown in jail.
before being transported across the states.
Their I95 immigration slips carried by all seamen while in the US had be surrendered meaning they could no go ashore during the two days in port.

As the day drew to evening we had dinner,shower and shoved off ashore for the evening.
Tony,one of the lads got up to get a round in ,when the door flew open and in walked Michael and Richie,
"Are you guys insane you could get in serious trouble?" Tony remarked.
"Totally insane mate ,but heck who 's going to tell right?
 Richie turned to Michael saying "Come on get em in we have some catching up to do right?"The first glass of beer never touched the sides before they ordered again and came and sat down.

 For the next few evening they slipped ashore around 2200hrs and painted the town

Now the young Third Mate,had no idea. they had skipped. He had been put in charge to ensure they did not gone ashore.
So when it came ready to sail and those two Welsh crazies were nowhere to be found aboard,all hell broke loose.
First the Third mate ,got it in the neck. First from the Mate, then the Skipper.
 With the ships pilot on board ,gangway was hoisted and stowed.
The Captain was not about to have the same problem as there was in Tampa.

But no one had told that to Richie and Michael,who right on time came back six sheets to the wind. gangway was lowered and we watched the Chief rush down to
the gangway and three steps at a time ran down almost tripping at the bottom and made a grab for Richie,and missed falling forward and the three fell in a heap. on the quay.
 To a cheer from us on the foredeck. Captain was looking down from his reaction of ripping off his cap and throwing to the deck shouting "Mr Toucher, what in heavens name are you playing at ? Get those men aboard now".
 Michael,staggered we all thought he was going to fall in to the water ,when Richie grabbed him and pulled him away from the edge of the quay.
 Michael then shouted "Hey you old fart" then threw a left hook at the Chief, but missed by a long chalk. Then slurring his words Michael trying to stand still was heard to say.
"Look, yea you boyo"pointing to the bridge ."Listen up we have come to an agreement as the cowboy thing didn't work out ...thought we would volunteer and become

astronauts"

Have to say that was the funniest thing I had heard and along with everyone else just cracked up,sure top become cowboys.

but seriously they were two of our own so decide to do something.

So along with Tony, we went down the gangway, told the Chief to back off and disappear.

But before we got to them the Captain was heard to say. "Mr Owen, look at yourself man. Your almost fifty years old, who would want you as an astronaut seriously?"

"And as for you Mr Jones, from what I gather you have been in orbit since coming aboard my ship?

A little talking and both agree to let us take the abroad. As we went up the gangway Richie said "You know mate NASA,needs people like us"!

Why's that Richie? I said, grabbing him as he fell backwards laughing.

"Simple! they need guys with a bit of bottle like us to go fly around in those dustbin lawnmower thingies they lob into space"

"Ain't that right Michael me old China ?

"Sure we're the right stuff boyo,we gotta lot of bottle"

Stopping at the head of the gangway reaching in to his back pocket "Just remembered! bottle have this half bottle of Seagram's,Anybody fancy a dram.

A two days sailing saw us in New Orleans. So anything could happen and it did. The two Welsh lads were sent home. So ended the saga of those budding Welsh cowboys and astronauts.

An Alaskan Moment

SPARKPLUGS,SOAP POWDER AND A SEAGULL

JAMAICA
1977

It was a time,a bad time to be honest,having been to the Island of Jamaica many times over the years.,but the country was not like before. You could see it in the faces of the people,the hard times had hit people hard. The highest unemployment,inflation had skyrocketed banging on everyone's pocket. Even the familiar blue beat Reggie had faded somewhat.
The ship had been at anchor over a week,when going ashore always had something like soap,laundry detergent which was given as a gesture.
I had always found the Jamaican people warm and friendly-very open,so during these hard times what little I could do to help was well received.
I had a friend Lloyd, a Rasta, stood six four in bare feet,amazing dreadlocks and a great smile.
It was his mother Mrs Nelson,who was the sole benefactor of my supplies my payment was always a wonderful smile and a big hug.

Lloyd, had a job in the Blue Mountains, working on a coffee plantation,one of the lucky ones
On his time off we would catchup along with a few of his friends sitting outback under a mango tree on an old rusting spring bed sharing some wicked Ganga pasting time in idle conversation and laughing a lot in good company.

As the days passed in Savannah la Mar, Time was spent down on the beach where he kept a small clinker built boat we would spend the afternoons scraping the hull. while sipping Red Stripe beer and smoking.
He asked me if I came across a reconditioned outboard, cheap could I get it. Promise him I would keep my eyes open.

A month later found myself in New Orleans, got talking to some guys who gave me an address of a place that sold outboard motors. So after a few beer s,caught a cab to the address. after a bit of haggling had my self a nice Seagull outboard for 70 dollars. Knew Lloyd would be happy and he would be out night fishing bringing in a little more money for his parents.
At the same time went to a huge American Superstore, to get a few things. They sold everything from Fruit of the Loom,,furnishings to well about anything.
Picked a few giant packets of laundry powder and packs of spark-plug's .
On returning to Savannah La Mar,
I drew the low card to do nightwatchman,which I really didn't mind ,meant I could get ashore during the days while at anchor. suited me just fine.

Evening were warm so gave me time to sit and read after walking around checking hatches and all was fine.
Managed to get through 'Across the Plains' by Robert L Stevenson, Herman Melville's,'Benito Cereno', and a funny parody of the 'Hobbit' which had me laughing in the early hours,
Mrs Nelson ,was over the moon with the large boxes of powder as was Mr Nelson when he saw the packets of spark plugs on the kitchen table,he would be king among his friends. Car spark plugs were more valuable than gold at that time.
To which I received the firmest handshake ever, along with the biggest smile.

Waiting for Lloyd, to return home that evening and finding his Seagull outboard leaning against the door.
I kid you not, have you ever seen a six foot four Rasta, with eyes a big as saucers do a backflip dreadlocks whipping the air then pick up a outboard above his head and do a dance. it was worth it. all that afternoon I lost count how many times he threw his long arms around my shoulders thanking me,
around six that evening he fixed it to the boat and took me out to the ship.
Waving he took off singing for a nights fishing.

That evening they loaded raw sugar from barges all night with not the biggest grab down the hatches while gangs bare-backed trimmed the bulk sugar in to the recesses.
They were not young men either most looked old enough to be pensioners,watching them from up top there was the most familiar smell of them smoking Ganga drifted on the humid warm evening airs
It was the old shoreside nightwatchman who told "You know the only thing they can't refine from raw sugar is glass my friend"
Guess the time I had seen those old chap trimming the sugar then taking a leak really didn't matter then....
Among my rounds was to check the hawsers pipes to which a couple of fire hoses had been rigged in case locals climbed the anchor cable and tried to sneak on board
to which a good soaking was waiting for the unsuspecting. But it never happened.

Around 0530hrs,I would swing out the small dory,and bring it to the gangway and ready it for the Skipper and Chief Engineer , to go off for a bit of fishing and collect any lobsters /crabs, they may have caught in their pots. Ships Cook,Second Cook/baker and Galley boy were called at 0630 to prepare breakfast ,then stewards and deck lads at 0700 for a 0800hrs start.

Many a morning, sat on deck with a mug of tea I notice a few sharks slipping by the stern heading for deeper waters, But that didn't stop a few mad crazy buggers from taking a dip from the gangway.
That was until Mac, the Ships Cook would step out the galley ,see them swimming then shout at the top of his voice "Shark". Then crease up watching them swim like hell for the gangway.
It was Sunday, Lloyd had come by with a good catch to take me ashore. close to the beach was a tin corrugated red roof chapel and people dressed to the nines were heading

for church,women and children in flowery dresses and hats with more flowers on them as the Chelsea Flower Show, Stand there watching those people filing into that chapel, who were going through really hardest of times still appeared happy smiles across their faces,very resilient then a little later listening to them singing was most uplifting that Sunday morning.

I had enjoyed my time in Savannah La Mar ,helped a few friends out and looked forward to my next visit.

Saying my farewell's to Mrs and Mr Nelson and Lloyd, we sailed south west for a port further around the coast. Black River capital of St Elizabeth Parish,then Salt River for more sugar.

Now we had a lad Len,aboard that had issues. He had already been mugged twice. And wasn't the friendliest towards locals,had a tendency to be a bit rude and had got himself in a whole lot of trouble.

One evening we had gone ashore and were playing bingo with some locals having a few beers.

When we saw the Len, come staggering towards the bar. we kind of ignored him as he went into the bar. next moment they was a lot of shouting. We got up went in and saw two couples Jamaicans standing one had hold of Len, getting ready to thump him

After one of the men explained Len,had threw up all over their table and food. And had started being rude instead of simply apologizing.

We could only apologize on behalf of the fool and offered to by them dinner.

But first we just had to get shot of Len and sent him on his way.

It was no more than ten minutes when we hear a gun shot,rushing outside it had come from down the road in which Len had gone ,so we lads ran in to the darkness and wasn't long before we heard muffled sound and came across Len sat totally naked in the middle of the darken road holding his right ear saying he could hear nothing. One lad had a small torch and turn it on to see a nasty burn on the right side off his head.

Later we found out what had happened... he was making his way back to the dock to get the boat back to the ship. And on the way back two locals had asked for a cigarette,but Len had told them to bugger off and call them something unrepeatable That's when they told him to strip hand over his wallet fags and lighter,and then fired the gun to scare him,then disappeared.

Took some time before his hearing retuned. He was a lucky fella.

A few days later the Mate, came down telling us we had the day off and a boat will be arriving and anyone that wanted to go across to a small island for a swim and BBQ. We all went.

Now apparently the atoll was used as a location for the film Dr No. The scene where James Bond saw Ursula Andress,walk out the sea carrying her shell wearing that white bikini.

After loading bags and bags of sugar stencil Cuba in large letters, were cut open and emptied before loading.

We batten the hatches and sailed for England..Another wake ..Another voyage awaits.

Tlinkit Indian Symbol

Drying Fishing Nets

DANIEL'S BUCKET LIST
1978

Not all stories are humorous,
 But this story of a chance meeting is worthy of mention.
 One can meet some extraordinary people who voyage by way of the seas
Even have the opportunity to converse, even for a brief moment.
Such as George Harrison,with whom it was a mere chance encounter one afternoon
while painting on the aft mooring deck. When I heard someone call out from the upper
deck,asking, "Possible to come down?". Looking up I saw and notice George and his
companion.
 "Sure,can you close the gate".
 Both came down he smiled and said "Just fancy a smoke somewhere quiet away from
the public you don't mind?
 "Be my guest"

I went back to painting ,but the first whiff of smoke knew it was grass.

We spoke awhile, then he handed me the joint, it was good stuff.
The conversation was about the reason for his trip, Which was to visit John and Yoko in New York and a business trip. No nicer fella could one meet.. Told the lads of my encounter and was asked if I had got a autograph. To be honest just the privilege of crossing paths was enough of a memory.

As it was with the actor Vince Price,who was a regular traveller in the company of his actress wife Coral Browne, who one evening came down to the 'Pig n Whistle' for an evening.
They were warmly greeted while Vince ,got roped in to a game of darts Tony a Baker and I sat talking to his wife. Shortly the conversation got round to cooking to which she informed us we should talk to Vince, as he was a very good cook.
Later,when he had done with darts he joined us, and his wife was correct he was in his element. To just sit, listening to well recognized deep voice and that smile was magic.
We had to ask him about his time with Hammer Horror Films and his other actor colleagues. To which in the voice from the movies he spoke of his great friend Peter Crushing. "Argh yes, the man that wants to die". Just that simple quote was a goose bump moment.

Again the opportunities while working on deck going about ones duty,one never knew who is travelling One day we were painting window frames on the Helicopter Deck behind the ships funnel throughout the day. The deck was full of passengers reclining in the sun loungers relaxing par taking in beverages.
After knocking off for tea then turning out to finish the job as overtime ,when we turned up on deck there was but one person sat in the middle on a sun lounger. wearing denim, a baseball cap reading a rather thick folder.

As we painted away the Deck Steward walked by and we heard him say "Mr Newman can I refresh your drink sir?
To which he,sat up calling to us "You guys like a beer?
""Thanks kindly"
The Deck Steward,was one of those long serving company men and heard him say "Sorry Mr Newman, I can't serve deckies.
To which Mr Newman, was heard to say "Jack, you get the beers and I'll serve them okay? Now there was a gentleman. Cheers Mr Paul Newman.

So one evening while on watch the telephone rang on the bridge. Being the Able Seaman on watch, I overhear the Second Mate, say "Yes Sir,,Okay Sir, Yes, leave it to me Sir. Yes, Goodnight
I went out on the bridge wing ,took a deep breath,the evening was still and one of those night where the skies were so clear one could see clearly every star in the universe.

Next the Mate ,came out and said"That was the Captain, on the blower, He has given a passenger permission to come visit the bridge during our watch. Can't see why he

doesn't visit during the day like everyone else .And I am to busy to show him around ,so want you to do the honours who ever it is okay?"
He turned the said " "Make it short then get shot ?
"And what about lookout?
'Just do it!
Just loved his attitude,an air of arrogance and very condescending,which I couldn't cotton to.
Around 0030hrs ,there was movement on the ladder to the bridge, then saw a young man mid twenties stand ing there short of breath.
'Morning, wow look at that sky ,that's something else ,never knew that there were that many stars you certainly have the advantage than us city folks? he reached out his hand
'I'm Daniel,
'Terry.
 watched him,he looked tired and drawn.
'Mind if I smoke??"
'Sure ,go for it"
'Want one?"
I shook my head. "So ,what do you do here he asked?
'm an Able seaman, watch-keeper, and helmsman".
 "How long have you ben at sea Terry?"
"Eighteen years so far"
'Long time"
 I was in construction ,until this happened"? Then he seemed to turn off and stood starring in to the distance.
' Any chance of some water mate?"
"Sure give me a moment,be right back?"
As i went in the wheelhouse the Mate, asked "Who the hell is that out there?
'That is the Captain's guest he rang you about,why don't you nip out and introduce ourself .sure he would like to meet you Second?"
'I don't have time to waste"!Was his reply.
 got a glass of water and heard the Mate playing his stupid game on his hand held digital toy.
\ man who was just to busy to say hello. Excellent.

As time slipped by I notice Daniel, was popping a lot of pills.
Had a feeling his health wasn't what he would like it to be.
Showed him the equipment used for navigation of a ship.
Had no idea where time went that watch,gave my relief a call at 0330 hrs.
Daniel, spoke about his 'Bucket List'.
 In the last few month he had rode across Canada East to West in a electric train engine,Had seen James Taylor in Concert and been introduce to the singer backstage.
His father was arranging a hot air balloon ride over the Amazon Rain Forest,
after the cruise.

My relief was on time at 0400hrs .so handed over ignored the Second Mate, and went below. for a drink inviting Daniel.

29

He was still popping his pills and in the light he didn't look well at all.
 So I just asked what illness he had ?
"Leukaemia, Myelogenous,chronic. bad hand Terry?"
 Daniel, was twenty eight years old and had weeks of life remaining. He wanted to
exchange addresses which we did.
for the remainder of the voyage we bumped into each other to which introduction
to his father .

I pick up my watch ,feeling a tad weary. No sooner had I got on the bridge, the Second
mate was on my back about the guest.

Saying "I didn't think he would take that long to be shown a few bits and pieces,Why
didn't you just give him the elbow?
"He wasn't royalty just some kid who had the Captain's ear and given special
treatment,you had a watch to keep Mister".
That's when I decided,well needed to tell him his fortune...
 "Okay Second ,you listen,and listen well... That phone call you got was the Captain
speaking to you ,not me.
He asked you, to to take care of his guest right?" And you never even had the manners
to introduce yourself because you were to bloody busy playing you hand held children's
games behind the curtain".
"That lad is just a young man,24 yr old ,has a serious chronic case of Leukaemia and
has weeks maybe days of life left.
 And you, couldn't be bothered or have the decency or the manners to just offer out a
hand to say Hi"?
He just looked at me then said "You have no right to talk to me in that manner Mister I
should report you "!
I looked him right in the face and said "Boy, you are really something else".
And walked way.
I did receive correspondence a month later from Daniel's father who informed me his
son passed a day after his hot air balloon flight over the Amazon Rain forest, and
mention his son wished to thank you,for a great time that evening in my company.

Old Panama Light Navigation

LONDON DOCKLAND CAPER
1963

It was during a time when the Port of London Docks, was the busiest. Ships of all nations filled
Its wharfs at times, two abreast loading and unloading their cargoes from around the world.
Main dock gates were manned by those friendly dock bobbies that waited for seamen with those baggage passes in which was fold a ten bob note, a little back hander to turn a blind eye to ignore those extra fags or a bottle or two over the limit.
It was said ,those bobbies, had bought their homes with those back handers.
This story is about such times.

The idea came about one evening during a session in the Kit Kat Bar Kowloon.
So on the early morning tide at the mouth of the River Thames with our pilot aboard we proceed to
the East India Dock and moored up. Nine month had slipped by since we had sailed that voyage
which had taken us to many countries. Now all wanted to get home to friends and families. Some of us would be down the Shipping Federation, Prescott Street,to turn around, sign on another ship and sail on the same day evening tide.

So after stations,it was a hearty breakfast,pack my gear which wasn't much just oilskins wellies,couple of pairs of jeans a few tee-shirts, cut off's, flip flops..most travelled light depending on what climate one was heading.

  Once signed on a ship told it was heading for the tropic's, but at the river mouth received a change of orders and headed north to colder climbs. Believe me standing on watch as lookout in tee shirt and cut off's and temperature going down as fast as a mug of tea.
But a concerned Second Mate, loaned me a coat and pants.

  Now on board we had this old cat whose name was,wait for it 'Cat-strophic' had been at sea longer than some. Been ashore in all ports during the voyage and always found it way back to the ship
 before sailing,
    And so easy to catch-just wave a bacon sarnie, fell for it every time,that old Cat-strophic,was so gullible!

 So here was the plan:
Capture the cat,pop him in a box and head for the dock gate,at an easy pace. dead easy..
But nothing is fool proof.
So cat snug, walking past warehouses crossing a few railway lines until reaching the dock gate a little way ahead. And seeing the dock copper outside his small wooden
 shed smoking then seeing me approaching stubbed out the fag and took an authoritative stance,shoulders back,hands behind his back...I expected him to slightly bend his knees
 and as I walked up and stopped, he would say those familiar word
"Hello hello,what have we got here?
But he just stepped forward and said "And what have we got in the box then lad?"
"Just the ships cat governor, taking him to the vet""
 Knew it hadn't been the best way for Cat-strophic,he had been shake up a little and knew if I opened the box he would take off.
But that bobbie just glared "Ships cat you say, haven't heard that one before lad ,just open the box lad?"
So placing the box in front of his size eleven boots,the moment I opened the box that old cat leapt out and took off like a cheetah across the African Savannah heading back towards the ship.
"Oops,sorry lad"
"Sorry really is that all you can say is sorry.?"
"Told you it was the cat .. Did you think it was contraband or something?
"Now I have to find the damn flea bag"
As i picked up the box the apologetic bopper wished me luck finding the cat.
I held my breath,It was all I could do to hide my laugh as I walked away.
Knew that old cat was smarter than the copper ,he would mostly likely be sat outside the galley door waiting for a handout from his friend the galley boy.

So here comes Part Two of our plan....

Returning to the ship, as the lads filled the box with thousand fags and a few bottles while I grabbed a cuppa and a smoke before returning to the dock gate with the 'Ship Cat'.

So it was off down the gangway a steady walk arriving at the dock gate and my friendly bobbie.

Who stepped out his shed."Well lad ,see you managed to re-catch your ships cat"

"Yes I did thank you very much"

"And believe me I ain't opening this box again so you can go whistle Dixie,mate"Go on be off with you,you cheeky monkey",

Once clear headed for the Eastern Hotel/pub. The landlord was always ready to take a bit of

shopping and paid well.

 So all I had to do was wait, have a pint. wait for the lads and share the cash.

Lamp Locker

AMAZON AND DEVIL'S ISLAND
1990

I had promise myself if I were to ever transit the mighty Amazon River,I would
sleep in a hammock on deck as not to miss the experience.
Now looking back, If I had slept in my cabin all that I witnessed I would have missed
so much and that would have been such a shame.
Approaching the mouth of the Amazon,one observes first, the blue water of the Atlantic
which is then divide clearly with a band of a yellowish brown of fresh water flowing
and merging from the Amazon River into the Atlantic,

My first evening while laying in my hammock on the aft mooring deck as night fell and
the small covered deck light shone,and within moment I observed many species of
moths and flying insects with an assortment of markings,sizes.
Some with transparent wings small and large,other so delicate wings of silver dancing
around the bright lights like that of small fairies. Then there were the larger flying
insects sounding like small fighter planes zipping by and attacking smaller insects and
feeding on their catch.
Many found the clews of my hammock a place to land and settle before taking flight
drawn towards the deck lights.
As the ship slipped through the fast flowing river and the banks of the river closed in,
calls from the forests wildlife could be heard like the call of a monkey to the grown of
a four legged hunter in the dense foreboding foliage.
Above the night skies dark and starry and half moon shone and reflected on the surface
like a giant mirror as one hears the splash of a crocodile enters the water from a hidden
bank in the darkness.
During the day,heat had one sweating as if hosepipe was attached to ones back;
perspiration was continuously running down one back and chest as one worked in the
open lifeboat. But then it was a tremendous viewing point
To starboard one could see clear to the north to the Guiana Highlands and Tumult-
Humac Mountains as a backdrop of greys and deep purple haze were visible.

The night again brought forth some amazing flying creatures,this time some with wing
spans as large as my hands and markings were just incredible.
Then I saw the orange glow in the skies ahead on the port side. drawing closer the
whole forest was ablaze,one could bull dozers tearing up the pristine forest. The two
hours that followed one heard the crackling of timber as the fires looked like hell itself
My heart was heavy at the pointless destruction. And thought how much unknown
diverse biology was being lost while the rape continued.
I had that same feeling many years before in the Indian Ocean, under the bows of those
Russian whalers amid the blood of those defensive whales.

The Amazon,is a dangerous river, sand banks shift through out the sessions and are a
hazard to navigation.

t was one morning around 0229hrs I was woken by a unfamiliar sound but had a feeling we had ran aground,looking over the stern, the props were thrashing and churning up the sandy slit. We were aground.
During the hours that followed the forward water tanks that supplies the laundry and much of the domestic usage on board was slowly discharged to assist freeing the bow.

Just after nine that morning, we launched the crash boat to do a survey and sound the river bed for deep water. Chris the navigator and I, were lowered in to the water with a audience of passenger on deck.
From our depth soundings around the ship it was as bad as first thought. Further out mid river there was clearance. Chris took the sounding, read them out,I wrote them down for him to relay back to the bridge as well as keeping the crash boat head up river.

My arm rested on the boats gunnel's when suddenly felt something touch my elbow . First thought a cayman common in this waters..But then, I saw three Amazon River Dolphins, bodies pinkish grey with long beaks and bulbous head
 This was a rare sighting as they are not seen to often even by the locals that inhabit close to the river. Who believe at night they change and become man, and walk among he villages and make young females pregnant. so are held in great regards.

I got engrossed in this playful dolphins,and missed a couple of Chris's soundings. explaining we had company, To which we were both reaching out our hand to gently ouch them when they rose up.
both lost in this once in a lifetime experience until ... the VHF radio broke into life and he Captain 's voice broke the silence.
his message was kind of jolly to which he said
"Gentlemen, lets leave the wildlife to David Attenborough,and more concentration on getting our ship afloat,which would be most appreciated?"
We finally made it and once the ship was freed .On our return the Captain was most interested in our encounter with River Dolphins.
Boca Del Chao, was a anchorage for any passengers wishing to get ashore. But there wasn't much there ,just one large straw thatched hut built on the high bank,a few adults and some children swimming nearby.
As for the the make shift mooring, that certainly wasn't built to cope with a forty five foot twin engine ships launch let alone a small dug out canoe was at best going to be a bit of good seamanship to get alongside.
The river ran fast and furious, so the art was to run up river against the flow then do a J turn, and steer for the tiny walk way jutting out of the river bank about six feet, which consisted of a dozen upright branches resembling a walk way no wider than the width of a normally built person, with a single plank to walk along.
t was some amazing seamanship throughout our short stay that it was not destroyed

   On board was an Brazilian ship agent , and was somewhat excited due to the locals had
aptured a rather large cayman crocodile reporting it had been killed ,shot dead and was ethered on the bank. later after a number of passenger had come ashore,the Deputy

Captain and one of our brave Coxswain, who we will call Barney. decided to knell either side the the creature... but just as the photographer, was about to take said photo,,the crocodile lashed its tail and all the rest of lads saw was a cloud of brown dust and two white uniforms disappearing in to the distant. To which there was much laughter.
Many of the crew had collected large and small plastic containers to send ashore for locals to use for collecting and storing fresh water. or other usage.

Ship,s Doctor and Nurse, came ashore and gave all a quick medical exam and handed over some medicines Out last port of call,before reaching our final destination,was Santarem. Manage to get ashore and walk along the foreshore the beach was littered with rubbish and old decaying wooden boats.,some could have been built during the 19th century
A number of families sat enjoying the sunny day, more children than adults it seemed stopped at a small Taverner,for a cold beer and watched a group of old men playing a board game. Wandered a little more then return to the ship.

Manaus (City of the Forest) situated at the confluence of the Negro and
Solimoes Rivers. With its long history,Manaus, was home to the wealthy rubber barons with their rubber plantations during the nineteenth century.
It is said,if one install a lion in their villa,another would water his stable of horses on champagne-a society of total decadence!
1,936 miles up the Amazon River,those early Europeans missed the society of their homelands,and built the Teatro Amazonas Opera House, bricks were shipped in from Europe,glass from France and array of coloured marbles from Italy. The artist and painter Domenico de Angelis,was commissioned to paint ceilings and panels
When completed it is said to have astonished the world-its equal to any at the time in Europe.
It is said,so its stated that Enrico Caruso, perform the opening night
It was not until the rubber seeds were smuggled out,their monopoly crashed. Manaus, fell into poverty.

For three days it gave me the opportunity to get out and wander. As well as just people watching from the deck of the ship.
People,many people carrying bundles and bags of shopping embarking the three tier decked ferries moored up astern of us.
Before the ferries departed,one couldn't help noticing how much they listed and look very unstable. On the lower deck it was a mass of colourful string hammocks and families. The between deck, was full of people and goods with the upper deck full of crates even a couple of cars lashed.

Throughout the day something that caught my eye,were boys and men going down under the wooden pier,then reappearing some ten minutes to half an hour later,this continued on regular intervals.
As the sun began to set most of the overloaded ferries had departed and the hustle and bustle had subsided below ,when from under the wooden pier about nine females of an

arrange of ages emerged from beneath.
As they walked by, looking up at some of the crew leaning over the ships rails waved at them,giggling and smiling.
I guessed what had been going on boys and men had been enjoying the pleasures of the ladies.

Later I strolled ashore passing the impressive stone buildings,and noticed the huge sandstone block each with a craved Roman number on each.
Nearby was a gentleman in an official uniform to which when I approached him spoken good English .So I asked him about the buildings.
To which he informed me the Customs House, Port Authoritative buildings and others had been shipped from London. He explain the stone was the well know Portland Stone, which had been erected in London Docks ,then each block numbered before being dismantled and loaded for shipment and had been reassembled during the nineteenth century.
I also found the splendid Opera House, all lit up, to which the following day spent a hour sat doing a rough sketch of the building.

Night life in the city was heaving crew and passengers were out and about.
Restaurants were busy and many were raving about the meal they had that evening, many had no idea what they had eaten. But the praise dropped by the second day,when it was discovered they had been served Bulls testicles.

There was one club name the 'Pink Pussy Cat', the entrance fee was ten bucks per person, which included a free drink, that from the reaction of the hardest of drinker observed spitting it out in disgust, saying it wasn't for human consumption,and more likely fit to fuel a tractor or even those rockets they launch from the European Space Station in nearby French Guiana.
But as the night wore on the bar got packed then the floor cabaret began. By a bunch of young ladies wearing very little and while dancing sprayed cans of dessert cream over them selves then flopping themselves across tables.
That was asking for trouble among drunk seamen.
Paddy ,my mate already wore a beard of whipped cream after diving between one young ladies thighs who wore a very skimpy bikini thong.
But the club bouncers reacted a slight to heavy one threw a punch missing Paddy, but Paddy's right hook didn't, then all hell broke loose, chairs ,tables drinks and glasses smashed. Girls covered in whipped cream running screaming trying to escape the fighting. It was time to exit.

Got myself on a tour through the giant lilly lagoons which was amazing.
Departing Manaus, the voyage down the River was just as amazing apart from the fires that were still burning to which angered me. To be honest I felt like jumping overboard and sabotaging those bulldozer in good protest fashion.

Devils Island,French Guiana.

Once a French penal colony where political,military and the worst criminals were
incarcerated. Devils Island is made up of three islands Iles of Diable,St Joseph and
Ile de Royale which lies seven miles off the main land coast.
In its time it is said eighty thousand prisoners served their sentence many never left.
It is said only four ever escaped the harsh brutal place. Malaria, Yellow fever and
Cholera,were rampart, both prisoner and guards died in great numbers,none were buried
in the small cemetery apart from early settlers and children. Prisoner and guards were
tossed in to the ocean unceremoniously,where sharks fed on their corpses.
Even as one walks around there is a sense of unease,the eerily,empty remains of cells,
now empty and vegetation has claimed the stone walls now inhabited by ghettoes, large
stinging hornets and snakes.,among the encrusted walls covered in creeping twining
vine where once echoed the cries of men.
 One underground cell with stone steps that led down to a arched rough stone roofed
cell cold damp and just standing in such a small enclose claustrophobic space ,rusting
chains still hung silent from the walls and the heat!!, one can only imagine what one
must have experienced being huddled together in close confinement with the insane,
sick and dying and its said that one hundred men could be held in such a small cell.
Outside in an area where prisoner were once paraded stand the remains of the structure
to hang or be guillotined which now only a plinth marks the spot.

A short walk along the grass pathway stands the Crimson Barracks,built by prisoners
now serves as a small hotel where staff from the European Space Station and soldiers
of the French Foreign Legion kick back for R&R. And tourist pick up a few post cards
and take a chilled cold drink out of the baking hot sun.

Venturing about maybe running ones finger over deep scratch walls of cells,it will
remain a place of lost souls and ghosts,
There is a chapel built of stone with a corrugated tin roof that stand as a testimony to
 one French prisoner called Lagrange, who spent ten years painting murals
and frescos upon it walls and ceiling. That afternoon as I stood inside that space I
closed my eyes and felt a presence.

Retuning to the stone built wharf I sat alone to reflect. ...then six large manta rays
broke the surface no more than metres from me wings outstretched glided then
re-entered the ocean with a loud splash. Then that was followed by the sighting of three
shark fins cutting through the waters between the islands.
During my voyages I would return to Devils Island another five times. But nothing
can compares to those first experiences.

A SLOTH STOWAWAY
1965

No one knew or even had any idea,where or how our visitor got on board,but there it was.

First, I heard was when the blocker(Bosun) pulled aside the curtain to my cabin.
Saying "You best come with me bird man"
"What's it about Charlie?"
"Think you going to like this one lad".

The name ' bird man', was due to me having looked after a few seabirds that had come foul during stormy weathers flying in to rigging or just needing care due to fatigue
At the time I had a storm petrel, in a box who was shortly to be released.
Arriving on the bridge there it was sat in the Skipper chair, looked like the creature was smiling. It was the toed claw that defined it as a three toed sloth. Normally found in South America forests.
Our only port had been Belém, Brazil, so maybe one of the local workers had brought him aboard and left it.

The old Chief said"Now that is one hairy bugger and slow mover,reminds me of a few on the department to be honest?"
The Skipper spoke "So any ideas what to do with it?"
"Could stick it on the 12 to 4 watch You wouldn't mind Second?"I said.
That got a laugh from those gathered apart from the Second Officer.
"He will well looked after Captain,just need a bath towel don't want to handle it to much, a towel was provide I was surprise when I pick up our new "Watch-keeper" thought it was going to be heavy.
The Captain,wanted to take a photo and took out a Polaroid land camera,and took a photo .
Then put the photo into a aluminium folder for five minutes,to develop. And then show us all.
I took our stowaway down to the cabin, to which the lads gathered around to see what

had been found.
I asked them not to touch the sloth and certainly not to give it any food from the mess.

It would just a few days before calling in Oranjestad, Aruba, where through the Radio
Room the Captain had requested the shipping agent to contact a veterinarian.
 It was given the name Cooper, to show our affection for our Second Mate .
During the day I took Cooper out on deck to which we rigged up so rope so he could
climb about.
Wasn't long before the Second, heard that we had called the sloth Cooper and was a
little annoyed when the lads started calling out "Come on Cooper. Move you ass"
 He was not well pleased ,but in a funny way we thought he was a bit chuffed that we
had call him Cooper.
Night time, Cooper,was happy as a sandboy climbing and hanging from the pipes on the
deck-head and sleeping at the foot of my bunk.
But let me just say,when that guy farted believe me it was evil.
Our arrival in Aruba, the agent had a car waiting,sat in the back seat we were driven to
 the Vets, lucky the waiting room was empty but when the door opened and he called
out
"Next" and stuck his head out to see the sloth and I sat there his mouth dropped open.
Don't think he was expecting to see a sloth in his waiting room!!
but the vet ,gave cooper the once over and reported it seemed in good health as far as he
could tell. While we waited he rang someone at a wildlife centre who would insure it
would be return to its rightful habitat. Said my goodbyes and returned to the ship
knowing our 'Stowaway Cooper, the three toed sloth',would soon be high in the trees
and among his own..

DANCING WITH BUTTERFLIES
1975

Turbo Golfo de Uraba,Columbia,is tucked away in the northern part of the country. We entered a bay surrounded by forest and dropped anchor. There was no signs of life. But upon waking the following morning to hear a lot of voices and noise being generated and stepping out on deck around the ships hull was a floating dock and barges and a whole lot of workers making ready to start loading.

A few days before reaching our destination the wise old Chief Officer ,had us lads securing everything that wasn't fixed or lashed down as it was well known that things had a way of disappearing if they weren't.
On the second day we heard a lot of shouting and went to investigate,only to find the Chief, along with the young Third Mate who was getting a blasting,as well as two uniformed locals standing on deck close to the gangway.
Now our Chief, was well versed in Spanish and from how loud he was we knew something had upset him and on a Sunday which wasn't good.
"What's up Chief?" We asked.
"Thieving toe rags they,someone has nick the compass from the Monkey Island"

Then he turn again on Graham the Third Officer."Didn't I say you have to keep your damned eyes open! What the hell were you doing and don't spin me a story.
I've been around since Noah lad,so I have heard it all"
About twenty minutes the two uniformed men came up the gangway shaking there heads.
"No find men who steal"
Really thought that old Chief, was going to boot both down the gangway,but instead he asked who had the keys to the Crew Bar?"Ships Cook this month Chief". said Ronnie.
"Get him down here pronto!
Shorty Mac,turned up handed over the keys ,the Chief disappeared and returned holding two bottles of spirits and 400 hundred fags, and thrusting them into the arms of the two uniform men saying. "Find my f...ing compass, you useless waste of spaces Now get looking and I do want results or your wish you had never set eyes on me? "

We really had nothing to do and this was entertaining. Another mug of tea and result we heard the shouting as the two so called soldiers one carrying a burlap sack and the other pushed and shoved two locals up the gangway.
The sack containing the compass was past to the Chief as he turned to look at young Graham "See lad these bugger understand a bribe...works every time,never fails, now go and lock this in my cabin."
The soldiers ask what was to done to the two men?"
"Handcuff the buggers to the rail until we sail".
It was one of the soldiers who said that would be three days.

41

The old Chief turned "I know when my ship sails man if they die of thirst meanwhile I'll toss them over the side myself". Now get off my ship".

Later I jump one of the boats going ashore,and took off .
 After a half hour found myself atop a raise looking down on a disused airfield,
the runway was overgrown it appeared to be long forgotten,rusting tin hangers now almost hidden by bush and trees.
        Sat under a lone tree giving enough shade I noticed a figure come out the undergrowth place a bag on the ground ,then watched him run the full length of the runway then
back then turned and ran back,five times I watched and thought who the heck does that in this heat.
Picking up my canvas bag I started down the slope to the end of the runway ,he saw me and waved.
Drawing close I saw he was a full blooded Columbia Indian,aged somewhere in his late thirties early forties.
Introducing ourselves he was called Mato,we sat a spoke about much I asked where he lived. About his family?"
 He wanted to know where I came from what I did .
 Then he invited me to go with him.
Having voyaged and wandered around the world ,never have I encountered any problem, and may I add there have many, many times found myself in some dangerous places, but as an old Victorian grandmother told me "Always be respectful of others! You won't go far wrong!"
Her advice held me in good stead throughout

    As we walked through the tall grasses we talked, Until reaching the treeline and a well trodden track. It was most welcomed the shade out of the shearing sun beating down, but the heat was making me sweat,i could feel it running down my back and salt from my forehead stung my eyes. Shortly we came to a river the water was crystal clear.
He made a gesture to take a drink and refresh then we sat awhile Mato, had hardly broken a sweat.
 I was aware of the silence around me ,just a trickle of water which was relaxing.
Taking a deep intake of breath I could smell the forest .
When suddenly from the out of the tall vegetation butterflies broke forth,some landed on the water as if dancing on the surface taking a drink.
Then Mato, slowly stood up,speaking in a low soft voice beckon me to do the same.
I watched as he outstretched his arms at shoulder length hand palms up.
Within moments both our outstretched arms were carpeted in the most amazing colourful winged
butterflies, I felt their tiny legs on my skin it was the most amazing feeling.
Mato, said they were feeding on my salty perspiration. Never had I seen such an array of wing colouration and marking some larger butterflies had wing spans the size of my hands Then noticed Mato, began to turn slowly arms outstretched his and mine covered we began to dance.

While all around and above in the canopy of the trees the skies were full of butterflies in flight As we slowly dance Mato grinned Then I realised I was grinning like a Cheshire cat from the magnificent sensation feeling and experience that I was so privileged to share and would never forget.

Feeling exhilarated we left behind the butterflies as we continued he kept stopping picking leaves and plants explaining their usage medicinally,once he pick a fruit to which I
thought was an avocado but smaller, he cut it, asked me cup my hands as he let the contents dip,it felt as soft as pure lanolin,explaining it was good for the skin.

.Finally we reach his village, met his family and a few other friendly villagers,share a meal and later Mato walked me back to the airfield.

At that time I had no idea we would meet again. A year later he saw me on deck and it was good to catch up,and was working as a loader,also he had improved his English. Gave him a couple of books to read. Had to mention dancing with butterflies.

It has always been an experience when going ashore and just bumping in to people, you never know who's path one will cross. Thinking about it. I have been like a ghost briefly encountering an array of people in many countries, walking many a dusty road, strolling a thousand beaches,slums village towns,and cities stopping to talk and listen to pass away the hours in friendly conversation, to learn something of those many people I have the privilege to have met..Then on a return voyage welcomed in to their home as a friend.

There have been so many,voyaging is not just about going from A to B or sights and places. Even the First &Last Bar, its about reaching out listening ,learning,making friends. Different countries with their own culture and custom is education if one is willing, just to understand that something one may do, can offend or be offence to others through lack of knowledge.

Now somewhat older in age,retired from a life at sea. Looking back, that well known song by that well known singer 'Old Blue Eyes' comes to mind. 'I Did it My Way' and I certainly have not a single regret.

Going to sea isn't just a job or a profession. Its was an education to see a world as it once was. Those many places that were once untouched and pristine, that now have disappeared and become over crowded as tourist destinations.

And now much is under threat as are our oceans and seas ,it marine life, fighting pollution and climate change,where many low laying atolls, home to generations of islanders are slowly sinking beneath the oceans as water rises.

Not their doing,most live a day to day life,unlike Europe or larger nations that consume world resources with ease and then discard with the same selfish attitudes.

While a planet cries out there are many that the most important concern is they can't get a signal on their mobile phone...seriously.

Now we face a different threat. But it will pass.
And may be, just maybe many will have learnt its not all about the latest mobile phone or other pleasures...Its about learning education being grateful for such a beautiful planet and realise,there is no where else to go.

The damage has been done,but nothing can bring back the loss of our wildlife species our mighty jungles and forests..But we can strife to work harder at stopping more damage. Mother Nature is willing to assist if we give her a chance to catch her breath: Remember Planet Earth is not a ship there are on lifeboats.

Q' Te Manu,Bora Bora

Passage through the Narrows

A DOG TAKES A CRUISE
1969

New York...Summers can be,wow!so hot,Winters,so cold those bitter winds that blow and whistle through those avenues and street.
But this story unfolds on one of those hot summer barmy day.
We had docked after another one of those twelve day cruises to the Caribbean. So I managed to get up town. A fifteen minute walk to Broadway and Time Sq.
Walking one gets to see life in the city.
People hanging out their windows with little on,families sat on the stone steps of those enclosed tenement apartment blocks,children play in the street cooling down under the spray of a fire hydrate during the summer heatwave,some play inside a derelict car that has no windows or tyres wave smiling as one passes by..
Smell of a local pizza take away drifts in the humid air:the constant sounds of police or ambulance siren echo through the city.
Uptown, its mayhem one just has to stop find a viewing point and just watch the masses in perpetual movement shoulder to shoulder,marching as if robotic. Almost like a giant ant colony all trying to avoid each other.
One can people watch and be most entertained. While sat eating a sandwich and a cool drink.
Traffic is as bad trucks ,vans yellow cabs jockey for a opening before light change,car horns blaring as steam emerges from manhole covers in the streets.
And New Yorks Finest standing on street corners twisting their night sticks or slapping the stick into their hand as the sunlight catches their badge of authority and glitters.

The many time in New York one thing I was aware of is: no one ever seems to look up. It a shame really as hanging from sides of those building and sky scrapper are some amazing clocks some very art nouveau and decorative.
Also looking up one can catch the eyes of office worker looking down,but wave and its funny how they suddenly step back out of view...then moment later appear you wave and they wave back and smile.

I found a music shop that sold transistor,I had a Lafayette eight track player I had blew a few transistors so I got a boxful for $6 in case they blow again. Picked up some art materials and couple LPs, stopping of for a bite to eat.

Now across the road from the ship,was the Anchor Bar,where most went for a quick beer, opposite was the Market Diner,which was always packed out.
That afternoon it was heaving shoulder to shoulder,music played ,lads were playing the table and to one side it looked like a toy shop a heap of giant size toys crew had bought for their children back home such as bears,lions giraffes and those Disney characters Mickey,Pluto.
A number of people in the bar that afternoon were passengers and guests to which one very well well dressed woman cradled a dog and was getting lots of attention from the

gathering petting and stroking.

Richard, one our lads on the Deck Department,was talking to the woman and her husband and was even holding the pooch. Everyone was in a friendly cheerful mood, until there was a big exit ,mostly catering department crew having to race back as passenger started to embark. Picking up their toys made a little room for everyone to spread out giving a bit of elbow room in the bar.
Through the bar window Yellow and Chequer cabs came and went dropping of their fares and suit cases. As the afternoon dragged on the place became more lively.
Now some of the crew had American girlfriend and the |Anchor |bar was a great meeting place.
One such lad ,was Danny Catering staff,he had a girlfriend and we knew he had agreed to take her to England,they had been together a while.
We heard sometime later she had gone to England he had taken her to Birkenhead which she thought was a dump and left dumping Danny to boot she returned back to the States. Writing him a" Dear John" letter broke the poor lads heart so we heard.

Sailing at 1800hrs as sun was low,sunlight reflecting off the skyscrapers of Lower Manhattan,and Empire State building,still the familiar sound of sirens rang through the city. Passing the Statue of Liberty it was a nice evening to put to sea once again.

Around 2300hrs we wee sat chatting when there was a knock on the cabin door . It was Bill one of the Quartermaster's on the 4-8 watch wearing just a bath towel.
Asking "Do you have a dog here?" ,Damn thing keeps barking?"
"No dog in here mate".
He left closing the door. But a few moments later we too heard a dog bark ,not loud but it was definitely a bark.
One of the lad got up to go for a leak then moments later put his head in "Heard it someone does have mute lads and I think its next doors.
 Richard had the cabin next door,so we went to investigate and as we walked in, there on
his bunk was that cute dog from the Anchor Bar.
"Are you mad Richard?" Dave asked.
"If you get found out,your in dire straits mate!
"What made you kidnap a damned mutt?"
"Seemed like a great idea at the time,lads..."

Twenty four hours later, Richard was on the bridge. The mutt, was handed over to the ships butcher, to take care of it welfare
"Why the butcher?, Well a number of passengers on transatlantic voyage would travel with their pets and on board were a small kennel area
The same butcher ,relayed a story while working on the Queen Mary,on it last Atlantic crossing a passenger had come on board with a great Dane, with saddle and bridle and a monkey dress as a jockey back to which I also had been on board that voyage and had been stop by the elderly lady and asked if I could hold the lead while she went some

where on the Promenade Deck. And would return shortly. Meanwhile passengers took pictures. Upon the woman returning some minutes later thanked me a gave me a tip of $10 dollars.

The butcher continue his story telling the lads,One cool morning he had gone to the kennels which had a stable door upon opening the top half of the door .in the night the monkey had escaped his confinement and as the door opened the monkey jumped out on to the ships rail then leaped off on to a lifeboat the did a nose dive off in to the Atlantic Ocean.

So during the cruise someone unknown had picked up on the dog story.

So by the time of our arrival back in New York. New cameras were waiting eager to get a glimpse of our so called stowaway and the reuniting with its owner. The pooch got the glory and as for Richard,he never got a mention, just something to tell his grand-children..

Cabo San Lucus, Baja of California

LIKE TO BUY SOME GUNS
1966

Laying alongside Pier One,New York,after discharging our cargo across the river in Hoboken,New Jersey. Long shore-men were now busy loading another as well a slings of large gas cylinders.

When the sling parted and everyone ran as they fell hitting the metal deck and fracturing some nozzles and the reaction was that of flying bombs flying everywhere careering in to bulkheads and bulwark.

The bosun was doing his nut and when everything calmed down he was straight over cussing the long shore-men, and them a right ear bashing.

The next few days they stayed well out of the Geordie bosun

Some of the cargo was Cosmetics,nylons and toys bound for the Central Americas

One afternoon we lads were sat around during smoko when Jock,appeared,big grin on hi face .He had a plate of Tabnabs.(Fancy cakes) Second Cook /Baker,had been busy making them for the Officers,but he had nick some. Tabnabs,are fancy cakes they serve to passengers on liners as they sit out on deck for afternoon tea.

I don't think any of us lads had ever sail with a Second Cook,who knew so many ways to make something out of bananas.

Once we were loaded and hatches batten down,derricks stowed we sail around 1700hrs. During the voyage south, we had lots to do two hatches needed cleaning Three decks to each hatch, over ripe bananas everywhere as then they were on stalks. Bimboards scattered every where like that children's game with sticks ,where you hold bundled in ones hand and then drop them and each player has to pickup without moving another, well that was what those Bimboards were like but down three decks. .

One hell of a mess,but we got stuck in hoisting up canvas slings full of ripe squashy bananas and dumping them over the ships side.

But the heat was exhausting work,sweat rolled off us equal to a sauna. And the further south got hotter. Believe me one could lose a few pound working in those conditions.

By the weekend it was all ship shape,so it was feet up and kick back,unless one was a watch keeper.

We rigged up a awning from a old hatch tarpaulin over three hatch,a few dragged out there mattress to doze out.

So there we were chilling when the Mate came down and we watch as he unlocked the Bobbie hatch, and go down in to the hatch.

We were a bit curious there was only cargo down there. Some twenty minutes later we heard him. First we saw the two brown paper sack appear,so went to give assistance.

To the Chief, appearing from the hatch saying "Hands off".

Norman, grabbed a sack and looked inside ."Oh I see,something for the wife,or is it the girlfriend Chief?"

"Looky here lads, ohhh, nylon stockings and cosmetics,been shopping then Chief?"
Reckon this would fall under "Pilfering cargo' what say you lads?"

"Should we report this to the Captain lads" remarked another.

"Been caught red handed Chief" Norman said, waving some packets of nylons
The Mate grabbed the packets,"Bugger off"

"That no way to speak Chief! What good for gander is good for the goose wouldn't you agree boys?"

He knew we had him by the short and curlies.

"Okay, okay ten minutes then I batten down"

.He was fuming,but we knew it would be shared out with his peers even a cut for the old man.

We all knew about his bit of skirt in Cortes.

But on the whole Harry Tate (The Mate) wasn't a bad sort really.

He had a sense of humour. Recall a crew quiz night,where the question was "What was the date and year Columbus sailed for the New World?". Someone said it was 1493 but not sure about the date.

Chief, insisted it was August3rd 1492,and wouldn't budge.

So the Engineer,who was disagreeing with the Chief,Asked."What makes you so sure Chief"His reply had everyone laughing.

"Look laddie, I know. First I have been at sea since Noah and when Columbus sailed,I was taking on bunkers(Fuel) in Gibraltar and saw him sail by,-and that was 1492.I even bloody waved". Had us in stitches. So not a bad chap. He was a bit pived he had got caught out pilfering.

As I stated earlier,one had to have a sense of humour,it really helped and back in the day even when got a tad rowdy,we had each others back. Sure there were brawls,at time got rather nasty a few I witnessed even Rocky Balboa would have gone for the exit. There were some mean folk around, there were many who had seen time in borstal. One I recall was called Mad Dog,after he was attacked by a dog and had killed it with his bare hands.

Another time we were in Djibouti. Horn of Africa, a quiet session in a bar when half a dozen French army guys came in bit loud and had one to many someone said something someone took offence and it kicked of punches thrown as well as a few chairs after most of us and they were suffering from cuts bruises a tooth or two littering the deck we called it a draw,and sat all together getting a few rounds in.

The French we later found out over a beer they were French legionnaires. But we turned out drinking buddies that day,all suffering bumps and so forth and loss of bit of claret.

    Another week saw us moored in Puerto Barrios. Guatemala.
Days were hot which made those tin corrugate sheets very hot and some who squeezed through to get to the bar in haste suffered a few nasty burns in some very sensitive areas which never helped their chances with the girls in the bars.

And when it rained on those tin roofs it cut out the noise from those loud jukeboxes from the bars close by.

    Now the skipper wasn't the norm hardly worn uniform to be honest he looked like a local in his grab. Even sept on the starboard bridge wing in a hammock under the awning with a stalk of bananas swinging from a awning spar. And was seen each morning either washing or scrubbing the bridge wing.

On occasion he would sunbath 'El natural'.

His Spanish was prefect and he knew many delict.,he had been running the coasts of South and Central Americas for years.

And was known to have a lady friend in most ports, In Puerto Barrios there was a Chinese lady whom he would invite on board and entertain.

The Chief would tells us lads she was off limits in case any one had any ideas?

But it was said a few had .

This this trip many had had certain goodies to sway and tease those dark eyed señorita's with such as a handful of cosmetic's or stockings.

    During the first couple days tied up....the ship,that is folks!!
Nigel and I had a job cleaning out the recess of the refrigeration spaces down number 4 hatch. Now they were dark spaces and were a good habitat for things with long furry legs like spiders...big ones .

Nigel, now he was a Cape Coloured lad and was rather hesitate about crawling in to dark spaces,so I went in to my surprise I came across a large cardboard box so dragged it out .

We found it full of toy cowboy cap guns and rolls upon roll of caps. So we stowed them away I our cabin.

Christmas Day morning, we were woken by a lot of shouting,so went on deck to find a whole lot of fellas with guns real ones seemed like there was some kinda of political coup taking place.

The train loaded with bananas had been sent away so had the workers .

We were informed we could still go ashore but needed to carry ID in case we were stopped.

There were soldiers on board at the gangway and ashore.

Said to Nigel,"Hey mate,its Chrimbo right lots of soldiers must have families young kids?".

Maybe we could sell a few guns get some beer money?.He agreed,

First, was to find someone and has it happened there were two young soldier like guys sat having a smoke on the aft end of the ship.

We walked up stood, nodded we both thought both men looked a mess their uniform seemed one or two sizes to big for their lean frames,even their helmet seem to big and any movement of their head the helmet would slip either one side or over their eyes .

Made us both grin looking at their rifles looked like old 303 bolt action .from their state looked rather antiquated and would explode if fired.

So it was" Señor's! Buenos dias!Como estas

"Want to buy some guns"? We have many guns!

They looked rather puzzled. So Nigel ,started to use his fingers as if firing a gun then saying "We have many guns, you want yes?Suddenly they both got up pushed by and we watched them heading for the gangway then down to the wharf and talk to what looked like a Officer, turn and pointing at Nigel and myself looking over the rail.

Next thing they came aboard and asked us to show what we had to offer.

Leading these revolutionaries to our cabin and drawing the curtain, pulled out the large box and opened it.. .

Taking one out, loading it with a roll of caps and fire it .

The Officer was certainly not amused,saw his hand settle on his side arm scowled,then left pushing one of his men aside.

"Guess that was a NO then Terry?"

But all was not lost ,that evening we took two pillowcases full ashore and every kid we saw gave them two each and a few boxes of caps. Once we got rid of what we had went for a drink. All that night the darkness rang out with cap gun fire going off.

Every port we went we gave them away to kids. When we departed the Americas and made our way home we still had many guns left. Avonmouth, Port of Bristol, there is a inner lock where the remaining guns were dumped

So at the bottom of that lock remains the end of our gun running days in Central Americas.

Pitcairn Island

AGROUND AND ABLAZE
FRENCH LINE S.S ANTILLIES
8TH JANUARY 1971

It was during a voyage through the Islands of the Caribbean,when on the evening of the 8th January,we received a Mayday call for assistance.
The QE2,steamed to wards the Island of Mystique, to the northern side of the island. Approaching, we could see the reflection in the nights skies the orange white glow and flames. Dropping anchor a mile off the distressed ship, the mid section of the ship was an inferno,flames rose hundreds of feet many passengers aboard QE2 had come out on deck as we launched four ships launches to aid assistance.

It was later confirm the S.S Antillies,had tried to navigate the shallow passage against the chart and struck a reef and had ruptured the fuel tanks. Passengers and crew had evacuated the distressed vessel and were said to be on a nearby Lansecoy Beach.

Before our departure we were informed only one launch at a time could get close enough to take on passengers.
But first, we had to navigate through a small opening through a reef and guided by a French Ships Officer, who would be signalling with a torch from the beach and for us to keep his light dead ahead and not to veer at any cost.
I had the helm and with Dave and Chris as crew. Rigging up the searchlight, when turned on we could see a single line of people many up to their shoulders in the water it looked like the beaches at Dunkirk during WW2.
One after another our launches went through the reef and helped the terrified people out the water then when full returned to the QE2 to disembark passengers to be cared for. Then back to the beach for more.
It took seamanship to hold the launch against a fast currant. While Dave & Chris hauled all sizes of passenger out the water into the boat.
Meanwhile some French crew, were causing panic by trying to board our launch by coming over the stern some even had suitcases I warned them to stop and called for calm but they continued to rock the launch making it difficult for my mates to get people aboard amidships.

So grabbing the boats fire axe went in to the aft cab and warned them if any one was to try and board and not wait there turn would be in deep trouble.
One person tried to board but when I brought down the fire axe on to the transom it was enough to stop anyone else trying. The picking up and taking all back to the ship went on all night. It was on our last trip back to pick up the officers who had assisted everyone off Lansecoy Beach and had signal and guided us through the reef.
As we left, I looked over the side of the launch and saw that all night we had been

running our launches through a reef with no more that just a few inched either side of the launches hull.

After being raise and launch secured we looked up at the hull and notice no even a scrape on the fibreglass.

With anchor secure we sailed at first light we anchored off Bridgetown, Barbados, where again launches were lowered and filled with survivors off the S S Antillies. And we took them right in to the town and dropped them in front of the statue of Nelson on the waterfront.

After they had all been landed ,we sailed again.

As for us lads on Deck, just another day in the life of an Able Seaman.

After a hearty breakfast, thought it was a day off? ,no such luck, such is a life at sea.

THATS NO CHIMP MATE,ITS A GORILLA
1963

Tramp steamers were once common in the 50s and even early 60s tramping the
world from port to port picking up cargoes to take somewhere. This is a story of one
such old lady that took us first up the mighty Congo Rivers second largest to the
Amazon River.

Our first port of call was to anchor off Matadi to unload part cargo,taking four days.
Then to Mdandaka,where we spent another seven days
The Congo can get hot,well more like screaming!
The metal decks could melt ones soles if you stood on the same spot to long.
The locals we had notice wore sandals made from the treads of truck tyres,hard wearing,
so we invested in a pair costing about half a crown. Lasted eight years until the tread
wore out.
Before departing for Bomongo our next destination,around thirty local Congolese native
board slept on deck and rigged up a 'Thunder Box overhanging the stern of the ship
which consisted of a few plank lashed together as a platform surround by a canvas
screen a make shift bog house supported by guy lines.

In Bomongo we loaded timber,hatches were filled and deck was stacked leaving a passage way to access the forward mooring deck.
Runs ashore were great but nights were a bit wild.
For a month were plied the river dropping off and picking up till finally we dropped of the workers and said our farewell to West Africa.
Crew were six on Deck, four in Engine Room plus officers.
Then there was the menagerie of the feather kind. Three Africa grey parrots,a Macaw parrot,Two dogs ,three cats. Someone said, there was a snake but no one had seen it for a long time. Not poison thank heavens,where- about unknown.

It was our third day at sea, when Harry, walked in the mess carrying a large burlap sack and sat himself down.
"What's in the sack?"Charlie, the Ships Cook asked sticking his head through the severing hatch.
"Bet he got himself one of those girls from 'Stanley's Bar,right Harry?"Harry slipped the rope and a head popped out.
"Its my chimp" Harry said smiling
"Jesus it a damn gorilla" another said.
"Nah, I was told its a Chimpanzee!
"Your kidding right?" Look at the beast, it has shoulders bigger than mine Harry"
" I wouldn't let the Old man find out" Cook said, before disappearing back in to the galley.
"Best you keep it hidden Harry" Paddy remarked, The ship was heading to Valparaiso.
Then one morning the Bosun, Surprise everyone, telling us there would be a cabin inspection. "What inspection, Ricky asked?"
"Cabin Inspection" the Bosun replied.
"Why?"
 "Because its his ship lad and make sure the alleyways are swept and mopped.?" As he turned the Bosun said and keep that bloody King Kong out of sight.

Donald, had been the longest aboard he had never heard the Old man doing an inspection.
Around 10.00, the Old man,both Chief Officer and Chief Engineer, came down the ladder, as we sat out on deck supping mugs of tea waiting. We watch them go into the accommodation.
It was a few minutes later we heard a racket the sound of galvanized buckets crashing about....then three Officer came running out the door almost tripping in a heap.
Guessing that was the inspection over Short and Sweet.
Even before we had finished our tea,the watch keeper appeared handed us a slip of paper which was written with a fountain pen. Just four words largely wrote GET RID OF IT.. Now that was going to be a big problem. We were half way across the Southern Atlantic. And only yesterday ,we had sighted the island of Tristan Du

Cunha.

The remainder of the day while working it was a tropic of conversation among all
to find a solution to Harry's dilemma.
 Some one suggested building a raft. Another was giving it to the ships cook and
teach it to wash pots and pans.

The old steamer wasn't the fastest, but she was sound, the weather deteriorated and
sea swell grew and rain lashed down for days we were thrown around,then on the
third day land was sighted and the mouth of the the the Rio de la Plata River. Safely
along side, Montevideo,was busy ships at anchor waiting or discharging their cargoes.

As for our 'new crew member,he was getting very playful throwing all out the mess
and scared the living crap out of the ships four legged animals.
It was decide to get our 'friend ashore. So a few lad rallied and found a old pair of
baggy denim jeans in the rag bag, a old holed sea jumper and a pair of size eleven
wellies boots.
Ricky and I did a bit of sailmaking and knocked up a canvas reeve cap for our 'friend'

Around 2100hrs it was dark, the port only dimly lit so our' friend' was dressed and
looked like any crew member in the darkness as we manage to get it down the gangway.
It would more difficult to get him passed any one at the dock gate...but as luck had it
the three men sat inside the building were watching a game of football on the
television,so we just walked out the gate and headed for any local bar.
First was busy and all lit up music blaring away.
Further long we saw someone exit the toilet behind the bar so we went in some one
remove the single light bulb and left our crew member in there and closed the door.
Then went for a drink in the 'Blue Parrot' across the street.
The follow day the ships agent came on board and we collared him and told him that
we had seen a large ape in the toilets across the street from the Blue Parrot Bar.
To which he said he would contact the proper authorities to ensure it would be
properly take care of. A day later the agent told us the ape had been found dressed up
and had been taken to a wildlife refuge.
But we couldn't stop thinking the thought of some drunken Dutch,German,English
seaman, nipping in that dark bulb less toilet for a quick leak and hearing the grunts in
the darkness made us smile at the time.
But it was good our 'friend had been well cared and looked after...But Harry did miss
his friend. Not sure about the Old man, which almost gave him an heart attack when
he opened the broom/bucket locker that morning...

Wooden boats and Seamen Rot in Port
THE GLASS EYE
1961

  Along the South African coast lie the ports of Cape Town,East London,Port Elizabeth,and Durban. Union Castle royal Mail ships plied the coast carrying passenger mail fruit and gold bullion.
During a time of Apartheid as a young man, something I could not understand or come to terms with was, Why was the colour of one's skin was so offensive to others.
 One voyage I had gone ashore alone,between the harbour and city lay an area of waste land At the bottom end of the the main city which ran right through its centre was Adderley Street full of department stores and the colonial railway station where many lads went during lunch for a few 'ticky hocks'. Now that was a drink some say were the dregs of the barrels and a ticky was worth 3pennies.
It had been know many would sit an hour throwing those small tots back then stand open the door and get hit by the hot humid air and suddenly find the loss of his legs as if they had turned to rubber which was most hilarious to watch and witness
 At the top of main street were the gardens and Cape Town university.
That day I found shade and a bench and sat myself down.

Shortly, I saw one of those Afrikaner khaki clad policemen with pith hat and large stick coming towards me ,then stopping in front of me then said "Hey you,move" in that deep Afrikaner accent.
I asked him simply "Why?
" You are sat on a bench for 'Coloureds only' now move yourself"
 I replied by saying, "'Oh that's okay then I'm white isn't that a colour?"
 He was not amused.
I was immediately arrested,and taken to the Police Station, showed them my ID card and said I didn't know sitting on a bench was against the law.
I was informed I could get twenty five lashes for such an offence
I was asked if I had ever been to South Africa before?" .Said no ,but I knew how things were in the country ,but didn't agree.
So I was released and sent packing. As I was leaving they also informed me even speaking to a Cape Coloured was a lash-able offence for sure.

During the voyage down the coast the Able Seamen watched over the hatches,while us younger deckies sanded and canvas the teak rails around the Boat and Promenade Deck or did some painting.
The African worker who discharged and loaded the hatches were known to be superstitious.
There was one Afrikaner foreman who had a glass eye and was known to take out his glass eye, give it a good polish,take out a hankie place it on the hankie and leave it on one of the crates and say to his men "I'm going for lunch now men, but you see I am here to keep an eye ,so no slacking"
And they didn't.
But one Able Seaman,would nip down the hatch and cover it over so they could take a break between slings
When lunch was over the foreman would return take the glass eye and pop it back in. none the wiser,

South Africa was certainly not a equal society had a friend who was Jamaican his idea of a run ashore was down the gangway a short walk along the quayside and then back on board .
We worked together and in any emergency that arose he had my back as I had his. But could not go to a pub or the cinema. He wouldn't even go to The Seamen Mission.
It was hard on the whole population ,they were banned from competing in International sporting events such as Rugby or Cricket,for many years.
 I was in South Africa again many time and in 1992 when they had a referendum I was in Durban and there was something in the air, a sense of excitement.
    I was to speak to many that day whites and blacks and when asked what the referendum meant to them it was a longing to play internation sports once again ,many said that with a tear in their eye. It meant that much.

It was a special time, things changing for the better,the days of unlawfully sitting on a bench or talking to someone with a different skin colour had gone and people like that foreman with a glass eye and his peers were gone. Signed in to the history books .

Male and Female Pelican

FOR THOSE IN PERIL
WELLINGTON NEW ZEALAND
10TH APRIL 1968

We had just finished breakfast when the weather hit the quiet Port of Wellington,the rain lashed it down. On board, reports were that the exterior doors on deck leading in to passenger accommodation were taking water due to the force of rain and high winds .so turning out to attempt to seal doors with towels,then we received a verbal message that the forward back spring wire had parted.,so we hurried to put out extra mooring lines fore and aft.
The skies were now dark rain beat down and winds were growing to very high rate of knots. Then we heard glass smashing which came from the cities waterfront buildings,cars parked close to the waterfront began to get blown in to the water. Wind just got wilder one was unable to keep ones feet, so went below to dry out.

Wayne,had his radio on and reports were coming in abut the Lyttleton - Wellington Ferry TE.Wahine' having serious problems just off the headland.
Next it was reported she was on the rocks off the foreshore of Seaton and she was listing badly boats had been readied for lower.
As we listened to the reports we knew that we should give assistance, so went to the bridge asking if we should lower a boat,but were refused.
The radio on the bridge was on, reports people were in the water now with 165mph winds a twenty to thirty foot swells in the channel.
Again we asked and said we would take a lifeboat whatever. It was then decided to lower.
 Now our boats were made of aluminium and open boats with a Lister crank engine. Chief Officer was reluctant about risking a ships lifeboat,but we lads just waned to give aid to those in peril out there in these dreadful condition. It was being reported the worst storm in 100yrs.
Six of us manned the boat along with a mechanic,in case of any engine kl-imps.
Once clear and heading out the swells hit us as did the wind and sheeting rain.
 Some time later the ferry came in view through the horrendous condition she laying on her starboard side. In the haze of rain and sea spray we barely made out figures on the foreshore in number hauling people out of the sea. On the far headland shore off to our port a number of survivors had made it to the rocky foreshore.
 Swells were huge, when a small open boat with a small cockpit some four- five meters bow to stern appeared riding the swell like a cork,then disappearing in to the void of the swell then riding up to the crest. The man started to shout above the wind and pointing to his stern where we saw someone holding on for dear life itself

63

wearing a life jacket.

In the lifeboat, the Chief held tight to the tiller we were screaming at him to get closer to the small craft but kept shouting he couldn't risk it.

So I grabbed my my Paddy "You can swim right Pat?he looked surprised. "You what?"looking at me .
He isn't going to get us closer if we need to get on board and give what ever assistance we have to jump mate!!
"Jump are you f***ing insane?
I took off my life jacket, it was one of those old cork block ones I was liable to break my neck if I jumped with it on. So there were were trying to keep our footing as the lifeboat rose and fell then grabbing each others collar we jumped. Not sure who was howling the most but looking down it seem the sea had opened up and below us was a dark void and we both fell in to it ,hitting the water was like hitting concrete. Then going under then breaking the surface as we rode the swell not more than a few feet we saw the hull of the craft and kicked out ,next both of us had our hand firmly gripping the side of the boat ,for a minutes we both hung getting our breath,that water was cold real cold.

Once aboard we went to the aid of the gentleman hanging on for grim death and tried to haul him over the transom,,he was certainly no lightweight so as the stern went down we dunked him under the water and used his body weight to bob him and as he came up we heaved and got him inboard. We wrapped him up and rested him.

His life jacker neck tie was tight and seemed to be cutting into his windpipe so paddy took out his deck knife and went to cut the tie,just as the man regained consciousness saw the blade panicked and bit down on Pat's thumb hard,drawing blood. Next we pulled out were young adults,then a young woman who we thought was in shock but was drunk as a lord.

The New Zealander, on the wheel was thankful for the assistance as were the survivors .apart from the elderly gentleman who suffered from hypothermia and passed away. We had no idea how long he had been in the cold waters,the hardest soul in condition can last 5-10 minutes before hypothermia sets in then any long rarely can on survive.

Making our way back we saw no sign of the ships lifeboat. Upon reaching the harbour authorities and emergency services were at hand.

We shook hands with the brave New Zealander ,not even knowing each others name we departed and headed back to the ship S S Southern Cross. Below now dry and warm, a knock on the door and there was the Chief Officer, with six cans of beer."Well done boys"
We told him to stuff his beers and reminded him. "Fifty one lives were lost today Chief,and if a boat had been lowered early maybe that figure may have been lower So keep your beer"
It was many years later I sailed into the Roads and slipped by those rocks at Seaton and Barrett Reef, I though of my friend Pat Reid, who had shared an experience during a time of those in peril.

I learnt Pat ,was killed in an accident onboard a tanker not of his own doing.
In 2016 I contacted the son of Captain Robertson,master of the ill fated TE Wahine
through email and related our part in that ill fated day.

King Neptune

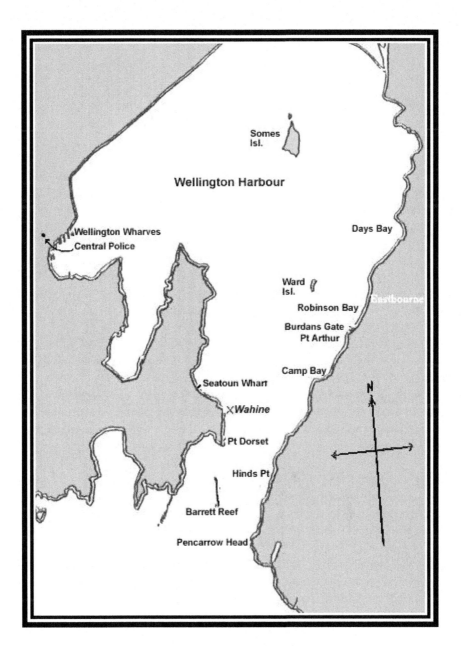

T.E Wahine founders

TAFFY'S PAINT DEAL
KINGSTON JAMACIA
1966

One sunny hot morning laying alongside the wooden wharf in Kingston. Our Store Keeper, Taffy,returned from an evening ashore and still under the influence.
He could be a grumpy bugger at times and was a tad annoyed we deckies had raided his paint locker.
The Chief Mate,had given us a Job&Knock Friday afternoon,so first thing Saturday we had turned out early,rigged up the Bosun's chairs around the funnel ,had given it a thorough sugi(soapy wash down) even before sunrise, and got it painted all before before the sun rose over Port Royal. 0800hrs all was squared away cleaned everything by the time Taffy,staggered on board.
So the weekend was our to to do as we wished.
During breakfast Taffy,was blurbing something about a deal he had concocted and was going to make a few bob. But when asked ,he just kept mum and grinned as he waffled down a bacon sarnie.
So Saturday night we all piled ashore for a night on the town, and Kingston was a place to have fun in lots of bars ,music and friendly people.
 It was around midnight we headed back music still ringing in our ears ,while a few lads sneaked off with their lady friends for a bit of you- know what.

 We were greeted at the top of the gangway with buff paint footprints which we followed in to the accommodation,that went all the way down the corridor and stopped right outside Taffy's cabin ,on drawing the curtain there was our Store keeper fully boot crashed out on his bunk and feet covered in buff yellow paint and out for the count snoring.
It was then we heard one of the lads saying "You better come see this lads"
So following him out on deck,we couldn't believe the state of the wooden deck on the port side it looked like a disaster. A empty paint drum of funnel buff rested against the fore part of the housing battered and its content cover the fore deck from the paint locker all the way to where we stood in total amazement..

 We decide it had to be cleaned up before the Captain and especially the Mate saw it.
So agreed,we first had to scrape up as much of the part dried paint as possible which

took an age,then a whole lot of white spirit and hard broom scrubbing and wash down,twice.

Then it was sand and holystoning, followed by a good bearing,twice then another wash down.

Oh Taffy,was going to pay for this mess.

 Lucky it was the weekend no one around only the galley crew who saw us stowing the hoses and asked what the heck we were doing on a Sunday morning scrubbing down the decks.

 When the sun grew higher drying out the port side teak decking it made the starboard side look filthy and we knew when the Mate saw the difference he would have us out there scrubbing and cleaning.

Looks like we had made a rod for our own back to cover up that damn Welshman's cock up.

 So Monday came around and Taffy was well sober,walked in to the mess and we lads just looked at him. then Barry,said "So that deal you mentioned? Make a few bob did you Taff?"

"What paint deal ?

"Have no idea what your going on about?"

 "Well we beg to differ mate show us the sole of your feet?"

"Me feet what for?

A couple of lads grabbed him dragged him across a table and peeled a layer of buff dried paint off his foot ,then held it up "This paint!!

"Guess you haven't seen the port side of the forward deck, it covered with a busted drum of buff paint your in deep crap Taff "

 He jumped up and rushed out the mess ,we followed him out. And saw a white teak deck.

 He turned "Oh that had me going lads thought I had spilt a drum?

I took him by the shoulder and led him to the port side told him to look over the side. Which he did, and saw the slick of buff paint in the water and clinging to the wooden piles of the pier.

Shit but the deck its so clean lads?"

"Indeed it is have you ever seen it that clean Taff?",Because your going to pay heavy we have covered your ass, because your mates here spent midnight to 0700hrs scrapping scrubbing and brooming to clean up your mess.

So your going to pay heavy for our effort all around the coast from the money you made on that deal that never was my friend ….. and he wasn't going to forget and he didn't, his wallet got very light over the next week ashore.

A JAPANESE SURPRISE
JUNE 1984

Some hour out from our destination making for Suva ,Fiji the ship received a call for a distressed vessel.

The report was the vessel was on fire and listing and required assistance.

So we changed course to give what aid we could.

The first sighting was to be a small Japanese fishing vessel but looked very even keeled.

We lowered a lifeboat and went across,drawing closer we could see no signs of fire,but the few crew on board were lining the deck as we came along side and threw our lines. Once aboard the small little Japanese Captain offered out packets of Lucky Strike cigarettes and smiled,other of the crew seemed more reserved and looked afraid for some reason.

It was only when the Captain walked us to the small wheelhouse and open the door And there lied prostate on the wooden deck of the wheelhouse was a bloody body face down not moving.

Then stepping in,the Captain,beckon us and opened a small door which as soon as it opened knew it led down to the engine room. He pointed as if he wanted us to look. Looking down the small metal ladder we saw another victim his feet were in the rungs of the ladder facing head down and a Japanese fisherman, standing over the victim hold a long narrow bladed gutting with a real nasty expression across his face as he whipped the knife across the victims chest then made a stabbing gesture at us as if saying anyone comes down will get the same treatment.

Closing the door we ask if someone could get a hammer and some rather large nails. Explaining we were going to seal the door and leave.

The Chief Officer,had remained in the lifeboat and reported back what we had observed.

With the door sealed and madman unable to get out we departed and returned to our ship .then shortly got under way.

Later, we sighted a Fijian navel launch past going to rendezvous with the fishing boat. Some hours later we were alongside, when on the jetty two lorries arrive full of rather large thick set Fijian riot police all kitted out batten and shields.

When the Navel launch came in towing the fishing boat and the second it moored the riot police boarded with haste,and within moments had the attacker in cuffs followed by a victim on a stretcher and other being carried off to awaiting ambulance.

Some passenger were lining the decks watching. A seaman's life can be very varied and unpredictable.

A Deck Seaman is observant,the longer he is at sea it become second nature. He spends eight hours on watch as lookout observing the horizon looking for ships and its navigation lights at night..he may notice a rope end needs a whipping or many other things throughout his day.

There is a well known saying 'Throughout ones life there are many teachers,who's path some cross and learn something important that can have effect ones life

As a boy,a Deck Boy,my first voyage deep sea I was to cross paths with one such teacher

He was an old Scottish Captain. Who I had never seen once for many many months I was aboard. Then one night on lookout on the Monkey Island midnight to four in the morning. Heard the wheelhouse door slide open, and then heard footsteps on the companion ladder.

It was a starry night and saw a figure walking to wards me ,then stopped not speaking but just stood looking out to the distant horizon.

I had notice the figure was wearing carpet slippers, pyjamas and dressing gown, He stood silent then watched as he lit his pipe. And I smelt the sweet aroma of the tobacco as it drifted under my nostrils.

"So you are the boy whose first voyage it is laddie?"

'Yes Sir"

'So tell me laddie are you one that upon our return home will rush home to your mother and never leave her side?.or are you one that see a life at sea and hear its call?

For a moment I did not reply.

I had grown up an orphan close enough, in care, foster homes. I had no one to rush home to. I was a kid and the past months on board had taken me far and wide,seen thing I only read about in books and I knew out there in the great big world were so many more things I wanted to see.

So I said to the Captain",A life at sea Sir"

'Good laddie"

He relit his pipe,leaned against the canvas dodger for a moment then straighten up

'Good "

"Now laddie let me give you some advice,and let me say take which advice however to will.

I listen to him that night under the skies full of stars never had I seen so many. His voice was low as he spoke.

'Now you may as you grow, take after some of your peers,not all but there are many who voyage this world and see it through the bottom of a beer glass and see little. And when it comes time to hang up their oilskins and settle themselves in front of a warm fire and decide to write their memoirs . They can tell you all the names of bars

around the world and how many beers one can get for a dollar. But forget where they went and when.

"On the other hand, you stand here on watch as an observer looking for that first sign of light on the horizon. Watch after watch your eyes grow accustom to the dark. You are an observer and soon it become like sense and you will realise your doing it even when you go ashore and in doing so you will see much more. You may meet all creed and colour and learn much in your travels laddie" And when its time to hang up your oilskins and sit to write your stories and memoirs. You will recall all that you have seen and done as if it were yesterday".

He turned I watched him disappear down the ladder and the wheelhouse door slide close.

For the remains of my watch I pondered on what the Captain had said

.Over the next few month without really knowing I had chosen the latter. And throughout the many decades that were to follow at sea it held me in good stead. Now I sit recalling much in a different country I have chosen to call home.

I like many still hear the call A man that goes to sea can experience many things if observant. Not only those amazing sunsets and sunrises around the world or those incredible,alluring moon lit evenings over head lands and islands.

How about those amazing starry nights in the middle of an ocean that reflect upon the calm ocean surface like dancing diamonds

Or a fluorescent sea and trailing ships wakes churning up the fluorescences as flying fish emerge and take flight above the glowing sea.

Or catching, with the right atmospheric conditions at sunset and the distant horizon, that not so well seen Green Flash. Or St Elmo's Fire during a lightening electrical storm hitting the top of the mast.

I became interest in life that dwells in our oceans and seas, as a young man barely a couple of years at sea time under my belt.

We broke down on the Equator. Only the humming tone s of ships generators broke the idle stillness. The ship rose and fell on the long low swell as I sat on the coiled mooring rope when there was a loud noise as if someone or something opened a air valve,but it came from over the side of the ship as I went to the rail as a balloon of mist rose up and the breeze caught it and drift across the deck and it had the most dreadful smell Then looking over the side was the largest whale a Blue whale, that nestled against the ships hull.

I was told by the older seamen it is rare even to see a Blue whale I wished at that moment I had a camera but not many did.

On watch on the bridge one could see many whales and dolphins sightings so I started to record everything I sighted and using my small hand book to identify species.

Soon one could distinguish the difference between spouts of the species. Then one would record number,species adult and juveniles,the direction and heading, weather conditions,sea conditions sea temperature,latitude and longitude, nearest land fall. Even off duty I would sit out in all conditions with pen and book to jot down sightings.

The oceans and seas are full of wildlife. Whale dolphin,turtles seabirds.

Once plying the waters of Central America ,between Costa Rica and Nicaragua. The skies were ablaze as if on fire when suddenly the sea erupted off to port,and in their thousands Pacific Spinner (Stenella longirostris)emerged and what was witnessed was the most incredible.

The colour of the skies now slowly changing to pinks oranges pastel blues and apricots reflected on the dolphins torsos and made a sea of rainbows. It was truly amazing and privileged to witness.

(And not a single one balancing a plastic ball on its head, being fed dead fish by some bikini clad cheer leader).

Through out my sea time I was never without a carbon pencil and small note book on my person recording everything I saw.

My time in Alaska, was seen through the eyes of a seafarer the scarred glacier rocks of centuries worn by ice, The forests of cotton woods and Sitka spruce that ran down the steep mountain sides to the waters ,waterfalls that cascaded with ease over untrodden ground where only brown and grizzles bears hunt in inlets for salmons fighting up rivers to spawn their eggs.

While Orcas navigate in pods in the dark waters, while bald eagles are heard screeching high in the thermals.

Going to sea is not all about work and duties it can be a education.

There is a saying "Not all men are born to go to sea. But the few that do find a home".

Once, I was invited to a dinner party,a friend of mine ask me if I could act as a courier, as I was stopping off at Madeira, could I pick up something that would be delivered to the ship on arrival from a old cellar in the city. To which on arrival a hour or so later I was called to go to the gangway. Where a gentleman was waiting with a wooden case to which showing him my ID and signing the recite to which having no idea what was within the box, put in under my arm to which the man who had delivered the goods almost fainted.

And said "Please handle with care sir, for what you now hold was bottled in October 1812, when Napoleon Bonaparte beat his retreat from Moscow.

I apologized,and carried it up the gangway and to my cabin as if I were carry a box of nitro. Placing it in my locker wrapped in my blanket

Arriving back in England, I was met and handed over the box and was given an invitation to the dinner.

It was a friend's sixty-sixth birthday and it was during dinner people were asked by our host to describe their perfect job?

Each person, related what that perfect job would be .

I sat listened with interest as each spoke,until it was my time.

To which I began.

"Picture a boy going to sea, and within the first two years had circumnavigated one and half time around the world,seen most of the known places and finally visited those far away island with bewitching names and many places unknown to most.

To have the opportunities to meet all tongues,creed and colour. cultures and learn something of their customs. To see the wonders of the world and to venture in the wakes of those great navigators.

Or just spend a day in the company of men such as Kaildo,a Tongan native who I met in the Island of Nuku'alofa Tongatapu, who next to his dwelling,there were heaps of giant clam shells that edged a plot of land beside his home.

The blackest clam were massive ,it would take two to lift just one shell, as one walked in the gate, at top end the clams granulated in size and colour.

He explained each pile represented one of his forefathers going back centuries as we walked past each, he knew their names. Until he came to a pile of clam shells "This was placed when Captain James Cook sailed on his first voyage to the Pacific"

And a little further he stop "And this pile was placed during his second voyage".

As we walked to the gate there were three smaller newer pile of clam shells,to which he told me one was his and the others were his two son. A family tree of clam shells. There have be many experiences. And that job was my ideal job, and I did it and didn't cost me a penny and for fifty years not a single days regret.

Our host came in with a bottle of brandy and opened it and pour each of us a glass then he asked if I would make the toast as I had been the courier that made the presentation possible.

So standing I raised my glass and just simply said "Here's to you Napoleon, Cheers"

Eye to Eye

QE2
THE SNORNER
1979

At the start of the World Cruise ,the Deck Department, took on four extra Able Seamen, So us lads who had been aboard longer were put in passenger accommodation so we had the comforts of carpet, beds instead of bunks and self contained shower and toilet.

Many cabins either side were vacant,so our first night at sea, we discovered we had been lumbered with a snorer. And I do mean a snorer,you could say as loud as any ships fog horn.

Just glad he wasn't my cabin mate

And when we confronted George,he wanted none of it kept swearing he didn't snore!.

"Look lads if I snored anything like you say,the Missus would have kicked me out the bed okay?"

"Well she has to be deaf,me old china ?"I remarked.

But like clockwork the following nights were the same.

It was Big Sandy,who said while we were painting on deck he had a Walkman tape recorder

So cue that evening after a session in the Pig n Whistle, It kicked off around 01.25 and boy! He was giving it full belt. So we crept into his cabin set up the Walkman tape,turned it on record and left the cabin.

During breakfast the following morning the mess was full,when we placed the Walkman on the tables and switched it on. We thought he might appreciate listening to him NOT snoring.

Sandy, turned up the volume. George just sat there "What's that bleeding racket?"

Then other in the mess heard and began making remarks such as "Jesus who the hell is that?"And "Hey lads, miss the farmyard that much you have to record you grunters?"

Which had many laughing.

"That you George"

"Bog off,are you saying that's me ?"

"Sure is George mate ,and you say you don't snore

He wouldn't have none of it, he slapped some bacon between two slices ,got up and left and told some steward sat close by "To go blow each other"

We arrived in New York,and passenger then occupied the empty cabins.

Back then we had a night in New York, so after work I nipped ashore,went up to Times Square,which can be most entertaining if one is observant.

Across the street was a Yellow cab,driver sat reading a newspaper,while two suits argued about who's cab it was and most coming to blows,a small crowd gather to see who was going to win.

Jack Dempsey's Bar and Restaurant, is a place where the boxing fraternity are seen going in and out . Was once running for a bus and bump literately in to Mohammed Ali,believe me like running in to a brick just said "Oops sorry mate!!" and carried on running just managed to catch my bus.

If one stands around one may see a famous face hurrying past,under the million lights and billboards,I was always fascinated by the billboard in Times Square of the cowboy smoking a camel cigarette and watching his arm lift take a drag of the cigarette and then the big puff of smoke disappearing in the night above the masses passing beneath.

Had some friend who owed a small Art Galley,49St,they would be away a lot had the keys to their apartment so would stay over for the evening maybe catch a show they were always leaving a ticket if I were in port. Went to Radio city once good show and saw the Rockettes Another show was 'Mame' starring Angela Lansbury.

I enjoyed the small little cafes and restaurants to grab a bite to eat.

Our snorer, well one evening after departing New York,there was a knock on our cabin door in the early hours a passenger a gentleman dressed in bathrobe asked if there was a way to stop the snoring ,We apologized and the man said "I wouldn't mind ,but its the wife you see we are seven cabins down the corridor and its keeping her awake". George finally volunteered to return to crew quarters So all got some kip.

Cook's Bay Moorea

GRISWOLD THE ARMADILLO
1978

Aboard we had this cat who had a sense of humour and a fetish for wet feet it would hide under the step leading from the showers waiting for its next victim to step out... Then it was an outright attack,we all got caught the tell tale signs were the scratches on lower limbs.

Now among our gallant crew there was one I believed hailed from Dover, Barry by name. A quiet lad lean and stringy whenever one passed his cabin ,curtain was drawn and one could hear him talking to someone,so we thought.

This carried on for some time and got all very curious. One morning sat on deck,land off to starboard a bunch of Frigate birds above us...Did you know their aerial marksmanship is spot on if one lies out to sunbathe and those blighter's are hovering you can bet a month wages they will crap taking in direction of breeze it will land on you. Never figured out how they can do that. Anyway Barry, came out sat himself down on the hatch with a mug of tea lit a fag

Dave, coughed, "Hey Barry you got yourself a pet or something hidden away in your

77

cabin?"

"Get away, I think he has a bit of skirt who didn't get of the ship in time before sailing from Hamburg isn't that it Barry mate?"

"Why do you ask? Anyway nothing to do with you!

"Oh come on Barry,we'll find out!"

"I see..okay guess the secret is out"

"Its a bird right?" Allen laughed.

"NO"

"SO what is it a cat,dog a talking parrot?"ken asked

"Nether,its a armadillo"I call him Griswold.

"Its a what? Did he say he had a armadillo called Griswold?"Jaz asked

"What the heck does a armadillo eat mate?"Another enquired.

"Barry looked at us and Said "Well let s put it this way lads you won't find any cockroaches in my cabin"

You should hire it out mate my storeroom is full of the damn things"The Ship Cook remarked, as he leaned over the rail above outside the galley.

"I do know about that Chef, its a bit shy doesn't like the daylight"

A few days went by we were all eager to see Griswold the armadillo. So we all waited out side in the alley having a beer.

When the curtain opened and Barry said we had to be quiet. As he said it doesn't like a lot of noise.

We all waited in anticipation. As Barry, got to his knees and looked under the bunk. We noticed the string,guessing Griswold the Armadillo was tethered to the other end. Barry pull on the string, "Don't think he's ready lads?"It was Webbie, who reach out and grabbed the string from Barry, "Come on,I'm getting thirsty?" Then he gave the string a good yank. Then stand on his ass mouth wide open and gobsmacked at what he was looking at. Then said "You are bloody kidding right mate,."That is your armadillo...a loaf of bread painted green and two button off a old oilskin for its eyes?" For Christ sake,I need that bloody drink now ?" Webbie got up and stormed out..

it was Saturday,we were restocking the bar, as we carried in a few boxes of beer Barry was sat in the far corner not happy.

Putting down the boxes walked over and on the deck between his feet were a pile if green bread crumbs.

"Who would do this Griswold wasn't doing no harm to anyone it was just a bit of fun lads? We couldn't do or say much ,but we decided to have a burial at sea. As you do

That afternoon a small group gathered on the aft end,Chippy, had knocked up a board. One of the lads dressed up like a padre with a cardboard padre collar who informed us it would be a double burial service. As a old greaser, had a worn out pair of work boots that had seen service and were ready for Davy Jones Locker, or a new home for a couple of crabs at the bottom of Indian Ocean.

As for Griswold fish food. We retired to the bar for a wake and lots of booze....

Tarr Inlet

MONKEY'S FIST

Pete,was a bit of a lad back in the day.
A few days out from Sydney Australia, we were busy cleaning scuppers scrapping loose paint and unblocking the small grating preparing for painting.
Pete was under number six lifeboat behind the boat winch when we heard him shouting and waving,so went to investigate. He had a handful of rubbish in his hand he had dug out the scupper pipe.
And in the handful was a ring,looked like it had been there a while and couldn't imagine how it never washed away,guess being blocked stopped it going down the pipe.
Pete,removed the dirt and in the palm of his hand was a nice ring with a sizeable stone and silver band.
"Finders keepers lads, the fiancee has her wedding ring"
During smoko, the discussion and theories was how it came to be there and how long?

"Don't reckon some chick found out her boyfriend was playing the field and got angry and threw it away ,thinking it had gone over board. Maybe a high wind the night and blew back inboard.?"

"Could be a jewel thief,"? Jock said. "Who stole it and hide it but forgot which scupper maybe" A few other wild theories were put forward during the day.
Pete and showed us had to be a emerald with a few diamonds and worth a few bob to.
Now Pete had a young lady back in Albany,New York and a young child and was wondering whether he should mail it or wait till we went to New York in a few months time.
So he held on to it.

The voyage around the Pacific was over, and we were heading for the Panama and Caribbean then New York.
During the crossing it was put forward he should make a Monkey's Fist, and hide the ring inside and pack it with rag or something as to stop any rattling around..
So in in his off time he did just that ,when finished he said he could get it through the US Custom by declaring it as a toy for the little girl.
And that's exactly what he did but didn't mention it to his fiancee. It was going to be a surprise later.
When she came down from Albany with the child to visit him. And his daughter loved it.

He look local leave and we sailed away back to the UK, and spent time cruising to the North Cape and the Mid-Night sun then cruise to the Mediterranean, before returning back across to New York.
Where Pete rejoined.
For a few days we noticed Pete was reserved and quiet,not his normal out going self so to speak.
So one morning in the mess thought it was a chance to confront him and ask.
We thought at first they had broken up or something.
It was Norman, who just came out with it.
"Pete what's the problem mate? You look like you have been slap with a wet sponge by a gorilla mate"
He muttered something under his breath,but we couldn't hear clearly.
"What was that mate? "
"Silly cow" We certainly heard that.
"Who's a silly cow Pete?" Norman asked
Pete took a sip of tea ,looked up
"Jesus ,your never believe it lads"
We waited in anticipation.
Okay I got home,all excited I was going to get the ring and give it to her. But couldn't find it anywhere right,so I asked where it was?"
"And you know what she said"?

"Oh that, just had to throw it out it got all dirty and sticky so I threw it in the trash,Fiona ,was so upset but told her "Daddy,can make you another one darling,don't fret sweetheart".
"Never had the heart to tell what was inside the Monkey's Fist. .Guess ill gain never prosper right?"

DAR ES SALAAM NIGHTWATCHMAN
1965

In Arabic, Dar Es Salaam means "Abode of Peace".
Back when we ran the East Coast of Africa Djibouti,Nacala,Zanzibar,Dar es
Salaam,Mogadishu and Mafia Island. It was a different time,unlike in modern times.
Life was slower,older and cheaper.
Having departed Durban ,South Africa. sailing out through the channel of the Bluff
where still the waters ran red with the blood from the whaling station and the smell of
the factory ovens and slipways loaded with whale carcass.
Was to be the beginning of my concern to act against whaling that would last many
years fighting to stop those countries that hunted whales.

Sailing north,the heat increased the only air entering the cabin was that old metal
wind scoop jammed in the porthole that never closed what whatever weather was
outside a thin gauze wire net fixed in the wind chute to stop those mosquitoes popping
in at night for a pint of blood while we slept.

We would be at anchor for days before going alongside. So it was, that someone had
to be night watchman, so cards were shuffled and drawn, low card had the privilege.
Luck was never in my favour, I drew a two of hearts.

Watch lasting from 2000hrs -0800hrs even when finally alongside I still had the duty. But alongside my companion was some old white bearded native local watchman, that had a tendency to nod off regularly. But he was pleasant enough
One could catch up writing a few letters or reading while sat out on deck ,it was warm but humid in the evenings and a extremely hot during daytime.
Walking about the ship when hatches were being worked one had to keep a eye open as the odd thing had a tendency to wander.

The Ships cook ,would leave out some food (Black Pan) for my breakfast, but it had to be lock away, as lads returning from a night out on the town would return feeling peckish, and were looking for a nosebag and my black pan was certainly a target.

Dawn was a special time and the first call to pray 'salate al fajr' echoed from the minarets that sent the flocks of birds to flight, then the call again before sunrise, which believe me those sunrise were most colourful.

It was the second evening along side around 0200hrs heard someone on the gangway then a sound like someone had missed that first step and a lot of swearing. Final a figure appeared at the top of the gangway as I waited to see who it was and it was one of our Trevor,and the way he was staggering was very drunk.
And burbling broken biscuits,which I could barely make out .
Sounded like he had come back for money to pay a taxi driver,waiting at the dock gate.
But the state he was in really couldn't see him walking all the way back to pay,so told him to get his head down and I would sort it.
So beckon for the old Arab watchman to follow me .first a bit of chalk from the darts board and proceeded to mark each cabin door with what time that person should be called from Captain to galley boy. I even gave him my black pan of egg, bacon, bread and beans and tea making things.

We had been in at anchor and alongside five days and I had seen the night life as yet so grabbing my ID and cash went ashore to find the taxi hopefully still waiting for his fare to return.
But getting to the gate there was no sign of any taxi. Walking that distance I might as well venture out to a bar being a tad thirsty.
Two full days adrift.
On my return I knew the crap would hit the fan... So better have a good story.
It was Frank the Bosun,who I bumped into first who said I would have to report to the bridge at 1000hrs.
To which on the dot I walked into the wheel-house to be confronted be both Captain and Chief. From their expressions not happy bunnies
The Captain ,sat in his chair "Well explain yourself Mr Cadet!

"Well,the second night alongside around 2am ,one of the lads returned six sheet to the wind. He said he had to pick up some money and return to pay his taxi.
But he was in no state so I advised he just crash out and I would sort it.

You know doing a good turn Chief?"
 "Good turn my foot you do realise you were gone two days?"|Remarked the
Chief,with a glaring look.
"Anyway I got to the dock gate ,but there was no taxi Captain, so I went in search".
 Do you know how spread out this city is Chief?"
"Two days, would you believe it I searched for that taxi ,but it was like looking for a
virgin in a brothel Captain"
That made him smile. But the Chief's, expression was "What time do we hang him
from the yardarm Sir?"
"I was just simply tried to do someone a good turn in my endeavour but failed and
willing to accept any punishment you see fit Captain"

It was the Chief,who spoke "So your telling us, you went running around Dar es
Salaam, for two bloody day to find a taxi and driver to pay him his dues right?"
"Dead right Chief".
Before he had time to say another thing the Captain intervened: rose and said.
Mr cadet ,as you may be aware I have been at sea all my life and believe me I have
heard a few yarns and stories...but I'll give to you ,that is a corker,in fact I would
simply state a belter"
He continued, "Now, Mr get out" As I turned he said ""I really don't want to see you
in front of me for the remainder of this voyage you understand.
 I noticed the smile as he spun around and walked out to the bridge wing.
Harry Tate the Mate, was just leaning against the wheel shaking his head in disgust.
There would be no hanging today.
Once clear of the bridge I had to chuckle then took a deep intake of fresh air.
Work Hard-Play Hard pays off.

ZANZIBAR COCONUT CRABS
1963

When your young nobody mentioned anything about the dangers one could encounter,apart from picking up a 'little something' from those young ladies in bar around the world and there were plenty with flashing eye lashes. Which many seaman for.

Now Zanzibar,there was still a sense of its bloody history etched in to the blocks of it stone buildings that was once witness to the trafficking of slaves and acts of horror as one wandered the the old city

Once held by the Portuguese in the16th-17th centuries,until being thrown out by the Sultan of Oman.

But this was the 1960s, things were very different apart from the mixture of blood that was most noticeable in the narrow labyrinth of streets African,Persian, Nubian even Portuguese.

Wandering through Stone Town, the aroma of spices fill the evening heavy airs, shops still plying their wears from brightly patterned fabrics from the east and eastern lamps to herbal joshsticks burning in many a windows.

While men sat around tables playing 'Baio' a board game, that throughout many Muslim countries is played which is said to where its played the rules can be varied .

 There is the remains of a building known as the 'House of Wonders' once owned by a very wealthy rich Arab, whoo dealt in Ivory and slaves back in the 19th century at the height of his wealth.

  For three days we were at anchor as were many other ships loaded with their cargoes ,some unloading into barges, Throughout the day was we worked over hauling blocks drifting sheaves and greasing running gear young lads from shore would swim out the ship and request permission to come aboard to dive off the upper decks. It was most entertaining as we worked.

Finally on the morning of the fourth day a pilot board and once anchor was up we slowly made our way to the berth and moored up.

Then that evening which was to be most memorable,not just the run ashore,but for the event that happened later.

About nine of us took our swimming gear to a beach where we stripped off and had a great swim.

Nearby some local fishermen were getting ready their boats for a night fish. To which they kept calling out but none of us understood what they were saying but they keep pointing to the trees where we had left our clothes and towels.

 We even started to think they were telling us there maybe shark in the water so we got out quickly. As we were drying off, a little way down the beach we hear someone yelling and could just make out someone jumping around hollowing. So ran over and saw the biggest bloody crab legs were huge had to be two foot,shell was large and had Danny's boot toe clamped in one pincher and Danny,was wearing it kicking out trying to get shot of the crustacean. Couple of the lads found a branch and attacked the crab and gave it a few hefty whacks,and it doing so the crab held tight then released but in doing so ripped the toe off Danny's right boot. Then there was a another yell but this time the Ship Cook was face down in the sand and on his back was one of the beasties . Again the lads whacked and hit the beast until it fell and made for the water.

The moon came from behind the clouds and lit up the beach and it seemed the beach were alive with the monsters.

Some locals nearby laughed at us waving their fingers as a no no. With everyone gathered up their belongings we made our way to a small bar nearby.

We were told by locals they were coconut crabs and were known to climb trees at night and they told us some people have been injury when the crabs fall on unsuspecting passer bys even dogs.

Needless to say we never venture on to those beaches again at night,only during the daytime during our stay in Zanzibar.

VOYAGE TO SOUTH GEORGIA
1982

1775,Captain James Cook, dropped anchor in the bay and claimed the island in the name of the King George.

For years the island sealer and whaling men hunted for furs and whale oil,almost bring fur seals to extinction, before turning to hunt the elephant seals for their oil.

In 1982,two hundred and eight years later,we dropped anchor to disembarked the men of the 5th Infantry Brigade consisting of Scots and Welsh Guards and the Royal Gurkha Rifles.

The SS Canberra had just return from a cruise and was requisitioned on the 7th April and sailed with troops on the 9th April.

Followed by the requisition of the Cunard Liner Queen Elizabeth 2, after a refit and the placing of two helicopter pads fore and aft she sailed departing Southampton12th May.

I turned in and missed all those flag and banner waving,there was no on the quayside waving me off to a war. Nor when I came home, I was asleep and woke to a ghost ship. Just a couple of MPs at the gangway to whom coming up behind them and saying "Good morning gents" which I kid you not, they jumped a foot off the deck in total surprise that anyone was still on board.

As most seamen know there was a lot of banter between crew of both Canberra and the QE2,with regards what their rolls were during the conflict. But each ship did what duty was allocated by those in charge. Canberra was in the line of fire,where the QE2 wasn't. That was the duty of the Task Force each doing their bit how ever small.

Aboard the QE2, life was as if it were a floating barracks squaddies were observed trudging up and down flights of stairs in passenger accommodation,huffing and puffing with full backs on their backs ....you can bet even us deckies would be huffing and puffing carrying two five gallon drums of paint. There were five of us on nights, four Able Seamen and a bosun's mate.

At first we did what we always done, washing down decks,maybe painting a staircase, That was until one evening,we we scrubbing down the starboard boat deck, and when it came to washing down a scupper at the after end by the stairs leading down got block and water cascaded down down the stairs and scared the living crap out of the men of the helicopter flight crew who came running out, all kitted out in the fire suits thinking it was a fuel leak from the drums of aviator fuel store on the Raised Boat Deck. Until we told them the scupper was block and it was just sea water. To their great relief. From that night, for the rest of the Southbound voyage the washing down decks down was stopped.

The ship stopped off in Freetown,Sierra Leone ,to pick up who or what before continuing on our way.

Early mornings around 0630hrs the Royal Gurkha Rifles,would be out on the Raised Helicopter Deck astern of the funnel for Physical Training excise. Which we watch each morning ,then as asking a sergeant would they mind if we joined in which he gave permission as long as we stayed at the rear.

A game they played was, dividing in to teams and placing rows of bean bags then each team had to see how fast they were by rung picking up a bean bag and returning to their team. The sergeant,who we had spoken to cheated and picked up to bean bags but got caught out by his lads and got a good old ragging,but all in good jest.

Another game was the Black Spot, which was to stick a sticker black spot on anyone and everyone without their knowledge and they were tracked by a single Gurkha armed with a rubber knife with stealth and cunning all good fun.
It was when the ship was at the point of no return the blackout came in to play. To which we on night's had to make sure it was total,and would walk around decks to ensure no light was showing,all deck lights were turned off as were navigation lights. So in total darkness when one steps out on deck it took a few seconds to adjust ones eyes. One evening no moon Richard and I were walking the Boat Deck, when we heard the sound of heavy boots jogging Then out of the dark void we were floored felt like a tank had run into us whoever or what it was we three went clattering to the deck in a huge heap winded to a voice saying"Jesus F**k where did you come from?"

Our human tank ,was carrying a massive back pack,as we all got our breath back he said he was a member of the SAS Signal troop. just doing some night training.
We invited him down to our cabin for a few beers.
During the voyage the brigade's padre,would post a notice each day 'Thought of the Day' on the board. Always something humorous.
Then the day before arrival in South Georgia he posted his thought for the day,which simply read. Gentlemen,as we have pasted the point of no return ,my governor and I have decide this is as far as we go and it sup to you now. So goodbye,good luck.
A padre with a sense of humour..
During the voyage a very large amount of those Kit Kat bars, were consumed by everyone and someone was collecting the wrappers for some promotion which evades me. But thousand of wrapper were collected.

Upon our arrival back in Southampton, and myself finding no one aboard apart from those two MPs. I went to the bridge and found David the First Officer, holding the fort,to which he was also surprised to see me still on the ship. After me explaining we coped for a couple ODF days .When the crew returned I signed off,only to find there was a train strike so I was going nowhere. So decide to pick up my camping gear at a friends place on the Isle of Wight. The returning to the mainland hitch lifts all the way to Lands End and picked up the coastal path and started to walk. Covering around twenty miles a day my tent was made of parachute silk with fly sheet a six foot ridge, I had a WW1 cape/ground sheet which made a great bivouac instead of rigging the tent on occasions.

The coastal path to my surprise was empty of people I saw no one .apart from at the end of the day if there was a local pub within distance.

Two occasions I had to get off the path due to fog which swept up the face of the high cliffs and made walking the path dangerous to close to the edge.

Another night after a long days walk of twenty three miles sun was going down and the last of the people were leaving he cove. when all were gone I couldn't help noticing the rubbish left on the sands and in such a beautiful setting. I couldn't understand why people were just to lazy to pick it up.

Then thought if they had arrived and found it in such a state they wouldn't have stayed and very likely move on to somewhere clean and tidy. But were so willing to leave their rubbish behind..

So I pitch my tent and spent a hour or more picking all the trash up,the retired to my tent . Shortly I heard a voice outside my tent.

He was a keeper from the estate some lord or other and the beach regulation there was no camping and asked me to move on.   Said I had recently returned from the South Atlantic and was walking the coastal path and had arrived and seeing the state the beach was in after the public had gone had clean it all up all the litter before trying to get my head down.

He didn't say anything and left it was maybe three quarters of an hour I heard voices and popped my head out and there was the keeper from the estate an a older man and woman who introduce themselves as Lord and Lady and were most grateful that a stranger passing was so concerned and had tidied the beach.

"My man, tells me you were in the South Atlantic and have just return home and even found time to do what you have done sir,Then I can only say a large thank you and you are most welcome to stay"

I thank them and said I would be gone at the break of dawn. And I was.

Walking the path was to unwind, raise a few bob for the building of the Lord Nelson Training ship, that was under construction for the disabled. Days went by till reaching Torquay, which I just went through and found a spot against a sea wall and making a bivouac got my head down.

I was woken by a flash light in my eyes and two policemen stand there. Again saying I couldn't sleep there .and again explained my self.

To which they really did apologise and left me.

Dawn had just broke and again it was the police,but this time it were two policewomen, who came bearing gifts. A flask of tea and two buns. Telling me their colleagues who had seen me earlier had told us about you and to look in.

I thanked them spent a little time while finishing the flask gathered up my things and bid them bye.

In all it took me ten days to reach Southampton then crossed to the Isle of Wight,then walked the seventy five miles around the Island in all covered 454 miles in twenty one days.

Two days later, I was back at sea feeling motion under my feet, once again back to normality.

HARRY TATE'S BANANA TRAIN EXCURSION
PUERTO CORTES
1964

Puerto Cortes, lies on the Northern Peninsula of Honduras,tucked in a gulf,west of the Rio Ulua River,its port is small a long wooden wharf with sheds made of sheet corrugated tin and a railway that brings in the wagons of bananas on stalk.
Behind the sheds are a string of bars handy for some to access by sliding the sheets of corrugate aside at the rear of the shed to squeeze through, instead of the long way around..
but this story bean one evening half a mile down the dusty road at a bar known as the The Lagoon Bar' appropriately named as it was built on wooden piles and hung out over the water.
Due to some earth movement a small earth quake a year before which had damaged the far end of the building which had kissed the gents toilet goodbye leaving only the green painted door that was jammed from the inside. So the Señorita's had become a unisex toilet.

With that aside the bar was always hopping and the girls were always very ,very friendly and music was loud.
Some lads came in later saying Harry Tate ,was in good form and had past him on their way down.
Then we heard his familiar voice approaching. When the louvred swing doors, swung open and in he walked ,well kinda staggered and made a bee line for us,at the same time tried to grab at a girls bum, to which he receive a hearty slap across the face for the failed attempt.
Now our Chief Mate, wasn't a bad chap. Alway gave Job n Knock if in port even a few at sea. But ashore he was trouble
We thought he had learnt his lesson in Guatamala. When he got really drunk and some lads had bundled him into a taxi,gave the driver ten dollar US to drive until the meter ran out then dump him. Harsh yes but...

Anyway that night he leaned on the table and in a lowered voice asked "Where's the bog lads?" Bursting for a leak!"
"Door on the left Chief" Door is really stiff,need to put shoulder to wood if you get my drift?" Tony said with a wink.
"Here keep your eye on me bottle I'll be right back!"
As he shuffled across the floor,he was trying to impress the ladies with his dance moves, tripped careered forward and went slap bang in to the door marked Gents and it opened and he disappeared in to the darkness which was follow by a scream... Then moments later a loud splash. Everyone was laughing. When the louvred swing door crashed open and standing in the doorway was something that resembled the monster from the Black Lagoon,covered head to foot in greyish mud and sea grass.

Then it started think those poor innocent girls learnt what profanity was.

It was getting late after a round we made our way back to the ship,but the Chief needed a drink,so nipped in to one of the bars we followed him in. Sat at the bar was Jock,with his double head silver dollar flipping for his beer, think every bar in the Americas had fallen for that scam. We kept saying one day someone is going to cotton on,but I wouldn't reckon anyone would be daft enough to take a swing at Jock, he was from the Gorbals Glasgow.
 He saw the state of the Chief,and said "What the hell happen to you Chief,you look like you have Crossed the Line and had a barney with King Neptune?"
Chief just sat at the corner of the bar "Beer señorita?" and downed it in one then slid off the stool and exited the bar as we went after him.
"Let take the short cut through the rear of the shed lads?" Someone said.
  Passing through the gap ,there was the train wagons at the rear many were already empty so we helped the Chief up into the empty wagon ,followed by us ,but the chief was knackered and told us to carry on and he would follow once he caught his breath. So we left him.
 The following day we were sat at the old dunnage table we built starting the day with a cuppa and chatting about the evening ashore when the the Second Officer, appeared asking if anyone had seen the Chief?
 "He was on the razzmatazz last night Second. And a little worst for wear so to speak" Jock remarked.
 "Don't reckon he went back to the bars and got lucky?"Tom piped in.
 After the Second officer departed.
We started to wonder if he made it off the train wagon,he was in a dreadful state.
It was Kenny and Sandy,who thought the silly bugger might have crashed out in the wagon.

For two days he was adrift.
One the morning of the third day,we heard the train approaching and we all went got up and waited.
 As the engine came in view there standing in the foot plate was our 'Harry Tate', and looking pretty rough and a bit dishevelled. The train whistle brought the Captain and a few officers on to the bridge wing. When the train came to a halt he stepped off the train and looked up to the bridge wing the looks on both faces spoke a thousand words.
 The second he stepped on the gangway we gave him a rousing cheer and clapped. Someone shouted "Hey Chief, been picking bananas?"
 once out of sight of the bridge and came on deck he turned and gave us the seamen farewell sign raising his third digit at us lads, to which we all cheered as he disappeared in to the accommodation. When the young Third Mate appeared "Hear the Chief has returned?" "Yes,Chief, has been touring the banana plantation. Guess he is writing a book on how they grow bananas and had to get some hands on research!"
One can only guess how he had to explain his absence to a very angry Captain...

Orca
Cape Ommannai Coronation Island
Lat N 55 29 12 Lon W 134 14 73

THE ALCOHOLIC BUDGIE

It was a point of discussion among us lads on Deck Department,whether to contact Norris and Ross McWirter, at the Guinness Book of Records,one evening as we sat having a drink in the Pig n Whistle,because we really thought Charlie Two ,warranted such recognition.

Here are the facts: Charlie Two, was a budgie. A companion to Charlie One,who was the Bosun aboard for many years. Now Charlie One ,had circumnavigated the world more time than many seamen, had visited most of the known ports around the world seeing them only through the cabin porthole. Had never had shore leave and was a known alcoholic to boot and worthy of being call a record breaker in any ones book.

Now, Charlie One, loved his dram of whiskey,as did Charlie Two, so one had a glass the other had a table tennis ball with an indent that sat in an ashtray with a small dram of Highland nectar. And both were observed on a daily basis par taking in the ritual.

Charlie One,would go to the Chief Petty Officer&Petty Officer Bar each lunch and dinner time and in the evenings. But having seen many who consume large amounts of alcohol will eventually pay for it in ones health as did Charlie One and had to go shore side to get some help.

Now, that meant someone had to fill the position of our Bosun and so it was but that someone was already know not to like the bird and was once caught red handed by Charlie One, holding the bird as if it were a plane and making out it was dive bombing.
So once moved it to the cabin the said acting Bosun, covered the bird and cage. For the duration as acting CPO. Only to give food and water,certainly no wee daily dram.

Charlie One ,returned,he looked well and took over his old job. But when he walked in to his cabin he saw the cage covered and removed it and to his horror in the bottom of the cage was Charlie, Two totally featherless and looked as if it was suffering from the DT's. Poor fellow
The table tennis balls was quickly found and a tiny dram was poured which was gladly received By Charlie Two,
It was some time before that bird grew his feathers and looked like its old self. But disaster was waiting....

The weeks and months went by everything was back to normal,but Charlie One started drinking again and again was seen staggering home in the early hours.
Then one morning as we mustered at 0800hrs to be allocated our work for the day, Charlie One, didn't arrive for muster.
Later that day we heard that Charlie One ,had a death in the family as it was relaid to us lads.
Someone suggested a collection and be given to the Bosun for his demise.
Then we were informed what had ready happened.
We thought, it was a family relative that had passed away … but it was Charlie Two.
What happened was Charlie One ,Had drank far to much and had found his way back to his cabin six sheets to the wind hadn't bother to turn on the cabin light and just crashed out in the comfort the armchair.
But upon waking that morning discovered he had sat on Charlie Two and had suffocated the bird.
Charlie Two,was given a burial at sea like many a good seafarer.
As for the Guinness Book of Record. It was their loss..
But Charlie Two was most worthy of being called a sea going lifer seafarer and now rests on a shelf in Davy Jones Locker as he should.

Christmas Island Kiribati

SPUD BURIAL AT SEA

1966

Burials at sea have been plentiful throughout the centuries through wars and peace. Even in these modern days ashes of loved one are still buried at sea.
During my own time at sea,preparing someone for burial is a solemn occasion:to enshroud someone in canvas.
There have been three occasions where I was called upon to do the stitching with a fellow seaman.
The person is wrapped in a light duck canvas and stitched neatly six stitches to the inch. Once done the body is laid on a thicker grade of canvas,where we would place pig iron bars/fire bars at the feet end these were used to weight the body then stitch the outer shroud.
It is said that those old buccaneers and pirates would put the last stitch through the nose to ensure the person was really deceased,so it is said.
There is a tradition of a payment given to the seamen who stitches a body and that was a bottle of rum which was forth coming. It was also witnessed on smaller ships if one went into the mess and found an abundance of fresh fruit upon the table it was a sign someone had passed away during the night and had been put in to the fridge in

the storeroom.. awaiting to be placed in a canvas shroud and burial upon the family back home was agreeable to burial at sea.

During one voyage,being a larger ship with a doctor aboard. Our ship had received a call from a passing ship their Chief Engineer needed emergency attention ,so in the middle of the ocean we met and on lowering one of our lifeboats went across to give assistance. It was decided to take him off and return with him to be treated. But after a few days he grew worse and finally passed away.

It was requested he be given a burial at sea as were his wish..Again I was called for along with my mate John,to do the job of sewing up the Engineer.
He was a largely built man and we set to, stitching him up in his tarpaulin jacket.
We were informed the burial ,would be held at 1430hrs.
A awning was rigged to give shade over the aft deck. The board was laid out to which the body would lie and covered with a Blue Ensign as the Chief was RNR.
At 1330 we carried the Chief out and laid him with the ensign. One end of the board rested safely on the ships bulwarks ,the other end on the small raised escape hatch that inside was a ladder from the aft end of the propeller shaft.

As we waited something took place that was most unsuspecting when the small escape hatch suddenly opened with the fixed weight,flew open lifting the board to an angle that the body of the Chief Engineer slid off in to the sea.
To which all hell and panic broke out it was no more that half an hour before the service... and we had no body.

Then the Second Cook/Baker, walk around the housing and saw us, saying "What going here lads?" We explained to which he just "Nah, A few bags of spuds is what you need boys?"
We just grabbed him and walked him to the stores,to which he refused to unlock the door saying "Come on boys, its more than my job is worth, lads the Chef knows what he has?"
But finally he unlocked and we took three bags and laid them on the board and draped the flag over all our hearts were beating.
On the dot 1430 a small party arrived,The Captain read the service, till final we heard the word "And we commit the body of our fellow brother...."
Pat and myself lifted the board waiting for the signal of the nod of a head from the Captain. And when given for a split second there was silence, then that was followed by three loud splashes ,which many ran to the rail and looked over even the Captain who had a bemused and a rather inquisitive look upon his face, before returning to the bridge.
It was one of those times when the saying "Stranger things have happened at sea "

JUNGLE DENTIST APPOINTMENT
1968

Hamburg, Saw the release of 'Superman' but in German, it was weird but funny as I didn't speak the language,however was entertaining.
Later went to the Reeperbahn in S Pauli,then did a round of the old clubs such as the Indra Club,star club,Grannies and Wagabond where one the Beatles had once played in their early days. Then it was back to the ship. The following morning grabbed a mug of tea and stepped out on deck and it was freezing,snow was falling and decks were a bit slippery. Just across the harbour,a Red Chinese cargo ship, was moored and along side the funnel was a huge picture of Chairman Mao. A few Chinese seaman appeared on deck waving those" Little Red Books' chanting the thoughts of their Chairman Mao.

Joined by a few other lads we started waving,when one of the lads disappeared returning with a handful of dog eared paper backs and we started to to shout "Thoughts of Harold Wilson" back waving our paper back copies. That was until the Chief Officer, shouted down from the Boat Deck,telling use to stow it to avoid a international incident accruing. But it was fun while it lasted and it warmed us up a little.
What a kill joy,but we had a good old laugh.

We sail later that afternoon, and made our way to the Kiel Canal for transit to the Baltic,
The weather was being reported as the coldest winter for decades. The decks were heaped like snow drifts. On entering the lock gate we moored alongside where a huge bronze plaque which declared that Kaiser Wilhelm11 officially opened the Canal from Brunsbuttelkoog to Kiel Holtenau, in 1895 its length is 55 nautical miles end to end..
Ahead of us was a frozen canal and laying ahead was a Russian vessel which due to winds had somehow block the canal sideways when we saw a whole team emerge from inside and each person had long poles and wrapped up warm started to use their poles heaving and pushing against the bank which the effort they were using showed by the steam coming off their thick clothing a good hour they heaved and push till finally they got line to shore and moored.
The biggest surprise was when those Russian finished most were smiling Russian women to which bowed to their effort and they smiled and bowed back.
 have no idea whether that help towards them going ahead when we got under way to break the ice. But those ladies never stopped smiling and waving at every opportunity as we steamed behind them through the blizzard that day and when we

finally reached Kiel Holtenau we waved those delightful charming comrades Bon Voyage.

Upon reaching Gdansk, Poland. It was frozen in as were we and had to go to Rotterdam to pick up fertilizer, urine in pellet form which smelt strong and made ones eyes water due to the ammonia. It also acted as a great paint stripper on metal.. but our cargo was heading to the banana plantations to grow bananas .

I started to get a tooth ache,but ignored it. Four days sailing my tooth was painful and the start of a abscess ,that became the size of a golf ball.

Some of the lads noticed and playfully said they could sort it one took out a pair of rusty pilers. Gave that a miss....

The Chief Steward played the ships Doctor with his medical bible ,gave me a few pills ,but I tossed them.

Finally we arrive in Lago de Maracaibo, to where a boat came out with a ships agent who had received a message to find a dentist.

Later I went ashore met the agent who had a old jeep and said he was taking me to a dentist.

Now, he drove so fast,hitting every pot hole there was on the dirt track and almost went off road half a dozen times I was lucky he did shake out my tooth even before reaching the witch doctor.

About an hour or so came to an a emergency stop a bit heavy on the brakes I thought as I held on tight. He pointed up a track "Señor, there!"

All I saw was a tin shed .

To be honest it was no bigger than a shed on an allotment patch.

So as I walked toward it a man in a faded denim bib and brace one piece came out .
"Señor, senior English yes?"

"Come English make good motorbike! Yes good.?"

He took me by the arm and to the back of the shed and there in cased in a concrete block was a old racing green old Enfield motor bike, it back wheel attached to a fan belt.

Which he asked me to kick it over to start it. Giving me a thumbs up,, as he went inside as I kicked it over, he stuck his head out the window. I was bloody curious what was on the other end of the fan belt so I had a peak and saw it powered his drill. To which ,now I have endured a few things like free hand climbing and falling a few hundred feet with just a few cuts. Being in the sea in 165 mph winds and 25 foot swells but this guy wasn't going to tackle my tooth. So made a quick exit back to the agent and his death defying driving to return to the ship.

Where I went straight to the Crew Bar, signed a chit for a bottle of Mount Gay Reserve Rum 12 year old,took a really large swig and told Robbie to get the Chippy ASAP.

So bottle in hand, sat down on a bench with two lads pushing down on my shoulder's and harry the Chippy aside my legs with his shiny pilers.

Taking another swig of rum told Harry to get it done ..

Next I was spitting blood and had a foul taste in my mouth from the abscess. Took

two more swig of Mount Gay,when Taffy,came out seeing me spitting out the rum.
"Oh no, now that a pure waste of good rum mate" reaching out to grab the bottle, but Harry,stepped between us and held up his pilers still hold a rather large bloody tooth almost poking it in Taffy's face.
"You next then Taffy,I m in business and the dentist is open?"
I even managed a laugh as Taff,shot off quick fast.

Back home some year later, I went to my own dentist and I told him about that jungle appointment and the ships carpenter and his pliers. He was totally amazed at the story. When in 1995 my wife went to my dentist for a check up, and he related that story to her, as he said he does to all his patients
My wife told the dentist "Yes I know the story well, very well, he is my husband.!!!.

Seaman's Church
Bora Bora

ONE IS MORE THAN ENOUGH,BUT SIX

As a boy in the village we would have choir practise on Thursday meeting at six o'clock, for an hour .
 Now the Reverent, one of those stone and brim fire preacher on a Sunday when it came to the sermon. Before the congregation turned up he would pick one of us to fill the water flask on the pulpit, but it wasn't water ,it was gin and through out the sermon he would seen to be someone with a dry throat and needed a drink of water. Hence why his long fiery sermons were long.
One evening we turned up for practise but the Reverent was late. So boys being boys out came the penny gob stoppers and licorice sticks and we started to explore the rooms and bell tower.
A few of us opened the door to the bell tower and reeled back, there hanging from one of the bell ropes was the Reverent who had wet his trousers.
We ran out of the church and went across to the pub to the small entrance the Jug & bottle and told the landlord who phoned the village police station.
.That was the first..

We were arriving in New York as we passed the Statue of Liberty,we open up two gun-port doors reading for taking on a gangway and a ramp for loading stores and taking on bunkers, Geoff was a young guy from the Engine Room, so he was standing by to attach the bunker pipe.
He was also our goalkeeper of our Deck and Engine football team and he was really good, In fact before coming to sea he had been a semi professional goalie,and had save our butt a few time with his skill in goal.
 That day we got told a larger gangway was going to use so we needed a threefold handy billy so went off to get one and grab a cuppa as we still had time before turning to get alongside. Leaving Geoff alone to take in the Manhattan Skyline.

Ten minutes later we return Geoff wasn't there,at first thinking he had nipped off somewhere ,when we notice one of the man ropes was trailing out the gun port door. As we went to retrieve it it felt heavy and as we pulled we saw a body. It was reported to the bridge the ship slowed down and tugs were made fast.

When the body was inboard it was found to be Geoff and a noose was secured around his neck looking like suicide. Question was why? How was it one moment your talking smiling then this we were shocked at his loss
 That was the second..

During my leaves I would have two days just kicking back after a long voyage then give someone a ring always got a job such as labouring with a group of paddies rough-necking, digging footings in all weathers, kerb laying on the new Hammersmith flyover, a bit of steel erecting,industrial painting, hod carrying on new builds. Anything to get cash in hand and keep me busy for the week on leave.

Got a job in DCA(Doughnut Company of America)a company that made sugar drinks and powder drinks and doughnuts. It was a night shift in the factory scrapping off the sugar build up above the cookers so no one else around. Start at 2000hrs till around 0300hrs then off home
. One morning around 0300 I had done what needed to be done .squared away my tools cleaned up and left saying good morning to the old watchman at the gate.
 Walking home I happen to pass the local Canoe Club House, and as I pasted heard a car engine revving away. Walking a little further something made me stop and walk back to the Canoe Club.
As I approached the car, I notice the hose pipe from the exhaust pipe,the saw a figure his against the window. Could not open the door, so ran back to the night watchman told him to ring the police and ambulance.
 First to arrive was the Panda car and two coppers who broke the window turning off the engine. I overheard one say to the other "Fourth time lucky Don?"
That was my third.

   It was supposed to be a happy time, a friend was to announce soon to be married and four of us were invited to a little celebration with her Mother and father who were caretakers to a small fire equipment distributors and live on the ground floor below the factory.
 All was well, seemed all were happy and having a nice afternoon .
 When the father, got up saying "Think I have left my glasses in office upstairs,won't be long?"
It was at least half an hour he still hadn't returned.
So we said we would go find him.
Went out then up the outside fire escape door was open,we went in and it was a large long building.
 Then we saw him it looked at first he might be replacing a light bulb as he was stood on the work bench so it appeared ,but as we got closer we saw he was limp and then notice the string. Yes string! Around his neck and the other end was tied to a A frame in the ceiling of the roof.
One moment merry,good company happy,Then stand, walk out and take their own life
The fourth.

 I was Second Officer /Security on board, duties were doing inductions in Fire Fighting,Search/Rescue and Survival among other things.
One evening I had just gotten my dessert ,when my radio came alive requiring my attention.
Upon reaching the deck and cabin many crew had gathered in the alley Chief Officer and Deputy captain were present and informed me someone had taken their own life. And bloody. Donning a paper suit gloves etc,went in to the cabin and saw the crew member slumped on the deck with a black tie around his neck which was tied to the wardrobe handle. His wrist cut as were his Achilles's heel.
The basin was full of paper towels and blood ,like his had a change of mind,but noticed a photograph stuck with blue tack on the sink at eye level of a Philippine female.

A young ship photographer,arrived to take some pictures but threw up the moment he saw all the blood and ran out.

With the the relevant evidence collected and sealed and given to the Captain for save keeping in a safe ,in case it was foul play when handed over to the police upon arrival in port.

Later I was told,it had been the crew members third attempt in two years. Once on board another ship and twice ashore.

What in heavens was the man still doing at sea?

My fifth

Then a week later another, he was bedroom steward,who was due for leave after his nine months,but another Philippine crew member had received new a family member had died and was granted leave instead. And the steward that had hung himself could not cope with the disappointment .so hung himself.

 Sixth. It must be a very fine line for someone to take their own life. And very few see it coming.

Shoreline Debris

ANYONE SEEN TEX

We have all sailed at one time or other with characters,there were certainly a lot around during the 60s and 70s. Such as those pure comedians,jokers,headbangers even a few worthy of a straight jacket,but characters all the same.

One I recall was nick named The Pink Panther, due to his appearance,especial when seeming him in dim light it was the posture. He had straw curly hair that look more more like a mane, his slim tall frame and he seem always to be leaning against the bulkhead out side the mess or crew recreation room at a angle legs cross much like that well know Pink Panther posture one sees on television.

Another was a older seaman from Liverpool. Called MacCanernie, pure comedian and those saying he would come out with such as if someone wasn't pulling their weight or putting their back in when doing something "Ive seen more strength in a pound of prawns" or "Jesus,you couldn't pull the skin off a bowl of cold custard mate" or once he had a real rough night and had crashed in in the crew bar and at 0800 hadn't surfaced that morning ,at 1000hrs we knocked off for smoko,he was still fast asleep when the bosun walked in and saw him all curled up on the seat,and woke him up. Saying "Hey Mac, Did get enough kip last night?" Mac's reply was simply genius. Remember waking for the first time that morning. Looked up and said "What

102

time is it?"

To which the Bosun,said "Just after ten,Why?"

Mac, just looked at him "Well F off it my smoko,wake me at 1030. One couldn't help but crack up, Humour at sea was priceless.

But the best was when the actor Telly Savalas travelled on the QE2 and he was in the Stewards Bar signing photos with his autograph..When Mac went over pushed everyone out the way Telly saw him asking if he wanted a signed photo,and Mac said "Be off with you whack, we just want your skiddies to hang in our bar. Keep the photo.

Then drag him over to drink with us lads. To which he got really drunk and in the early hours carried Telly Savalas, up the stairs to One Deck and dumped him on the carpet in passenger accommodation. Before closing the door we all said "Who loves you Baby.

Among our gallant crew, was a greaser. When we first saw him,he had come aboard dressed like a cowboy. We thought he was an American ,who had wandered on board to ask directions thinking he was lost.

Some of the lads got up and looked over the side down to the quayside. Then asking. "Where's your horse sheriff?"

But Tex, turned out to be okay,as the month went by,we all accepted him for who he was.

Not sure about the long serving Chief Engineer,who never knew what hit him at the beginning when Tex rolled up wearing a Stetson ,cowboy boots and a red buttoned down shirt. But he knew his job and got on with it in a professional way.

Ashore, he was just the same,and he certainly put away the bevies and if the bar had a jukebox box it was always Hank Williams ,Johnny Cash or other Country and Western singers, and believe me he had a great voice when he sang along to the record.

Occasionally ,when in Puerto Armuelles,Panama . We would get a lift and nip down to Volcan,not far from the boarders of Costa Rica. Now Tex really was in his element there and blended in. a dusty little place back then, Seriously a one horse town,bar saloons with hitching post out side and horse tied up some local carried guns. And wasn't it wasn't surprising to hear occasionally a gun shot.

After a night of merry making and meeting people the was always someone even six sheets to the wind was driving back home and willing to take a few seamen in the rear of their truck. Which was an experience in its self. The driver hitting every single pothole and at time going off road tearing the vegetation before hitting the dusty track again and more potholes. Wonder anyone ever made it back … but great times.

But then came that gangway there was an art to get off and on .as due to the large swells the gangway was operated by a crane driver who lowered it so you could jump on easy when sober, a tad harder if like some rat faced. That could be a rib ache and funny to watch.

I recall a time in port had gone ashore,it was raining and on my way walking into town with my mate Lenny,heard some muffled crying nearby and found two kids under some boards and tin sheet cold and crying.

I returned to the ship God knows what time in was?

And made my way to the Captains cabin and knocked on his door. Shorty it opened, he was wearing a dressing gown and his hat .

"What up ?" he asked half asleep.

And I said "Captain,would they be any chance of buying two ships blankets. Carrying told him "Found a couple very young children sleeping under some boards in a ditch,cold wet and hungry. Just want to help is there any chance of a couple of blankets Captain?"

He looked at me and said "I commend you on your deep concern lad,but its not place to sell ships store Sorry I can not . I bid you Good Morning" and quietly closed the door.

I went below grabbed my blanket then went to len's cabin and took his ,found some fruit and bread in the mess and hopped the gangway and took off back to Lenny and the children.

As I walked under the bridge I looked up and saw the Captain and Duty Watch Officer looking down.

I almost stopped and thought about returning the blankets ,but there were more needy,so walked.

The following morning I was varnishing the teak doors of the Radio Room,when the Captain came on to the bridge wing and he saw me and came over.

He just stood watching me for a moment then spoke.

"Mister Cadet, so did you get your dilemma sorted last night?"

"Yes I did Captain "

Seriously, I was waiting to be pulled over the coals. But instead he reached out his hand shook mine and said "Well done young man" And turned smiling...

Soon after we headed for the Panama Canal, that night we had film I set up the old Bell & Howard reel projector on the hatch using the freshly painted mast housing as the screen. It was right up Tex's street. Film starring Frank Sinatra and Dean Martin 'Four for Texas.

Tex had front seat wearing his Stetson. After the film, we sat around chatting. Tex disappeared ,knew he was on watch 12-4 so thought he went to get some shut eye.

But around 0024hrs a engineer asked if we knew where Tex was as he should be below on watch but hadn't turned up.

"Thought he was getting a few winks?" I said.

We searched the ship he was nowhere to be found a Anderson of 360 was taken and went back on our course but nothing. With everything back to normal we sat outside talking about the whys and wherefores when we heard someone whistling,sounding like the theme tune from Four for Texas... then again and it seemed to come from above us as we looked up we saw the leg and cowboy boots hanging over the mast table.

Shouting ,we got Tex's attention he asked what was going on!

He climbed down and said "Lads it s nice up there dead quiet...saw us turn we haven't got a change of order have we?"

"Did you know the ships crew have been looking for you and the Skipper ,did a Anderson Turn, to look for you thinking you had gone over the side .

The bosun turned up and dragged him away saying "Lad your up to your neck."

Next morning Tex,was up before the Old man. He got fine two days pay and forfeited one days pay Tex got a right bollocking.

Close Call

RECYCLING
1979

It started with those ring pulls on cans,got bars and crew to save them and wasn't long before I had thousand in boxes. When I had every space full. I contacted a guy in New York who picked them up took them away, weighed them and return the follow voyage and handed me cash..
Then decided what else was being thrown over the ship side that could be recycled and money made for a cause.

To get some idea I thought a man onboard who would know was the Chief Storekeeper. Approaching him and asking if he could give me some idea may be a list of what is supplied to all bars on board total. He was most agreeable but would take as few days.
When he gave the list it was staggering The total figure1378,404 beer and soft drinks can and glass bottle for both passenger and crew, not counting wine or champagne bottles.
I knew ahead of me was a big task. But someone had to change attitudes to a different way of thinking the oceans and seas were not just a giant dustbin, and what effect is would or has on the marine life. Much like the nuclear waste that was dumped in drum in the Atlantic and close to the coast in earlier years and Greenpeace fought for it to be halted. I included

.

|So first it was information posted about the ship were it would be seen. Also word of mouth to anyone that was interested.

At the same time I shared my knowledge about Whales and Dolphins, posting pictures how to identify different whale species by their spouts and dorsal fins. This also included marine pollution which was growing in our oceans and seas. And I could see becoming a very serious problem in the future by the craze for throwing not restoring or exchanging and selling. Plastics I could see become a very environmental problem

Even when I came ashore on leave. I saw the amount of rubbish in street and road around cities as if it was just accepted as the norm by local Councils

On board crew would stop and ask question and all seemed interested,many asked what could they do to help,It wasn't long before many spaces under stairwell we stacked with recyclables.

On board was a passenger Barclay's Bank and as I was already banking with Barclay's shoreside with my own money. Started an account on board which certain environmental groups would receive monies to help certain causes such as Greenpeace and the like.

Then I turned to the ships daily dumping and their was much that went over the ships stern.

The ship did a six week refit in Southampton in the KGV dry dock, and the after decks were head high in carpets ,underlay furnishings fuel drums expired medical waste even some container marked poison, There was even a twenty foot three tier stage steps along with much more believing it was to be land was not .When the Qe2 left the dry dock it remained littering the decks...That was till we sailed that evening too do a trail run down the English Channel where off Portland Bill in the darkness it was going to be dumped

I rounded up a few lads with large felt tip pens and asked them to marks as much as possible with large lettering QE2 in case it washed up ashore.

As for the three tier stage step which was thrown over board would float to which some unsuspecting fishing boat or yachts man would hit in the darkness and put life's at risk.

With that, I sat and wrote a letter which was copied and posted to certain people such as The Secretary of State for the Environment, at the time being Michael Hesltine MP. Along with others to groups it would concern.

I gave a copy to the Chief Officer ,who instantly filed it under G for garbage in the Rosie(Waste bin).

A little while later, I was in front of the Captain and asked why he had not see a copy. There were a few suited gentlemen present,a long with the Chief Officer.

I said the Chief had been given a copy which he has thrown away and discarded it he wasn't a happy bunny when the company got fined.

It was some years later pollution was taken far more serious at sea where the International Marpole Agreement came in to force controlling what and where certain articles could be dumped in deeper waters.

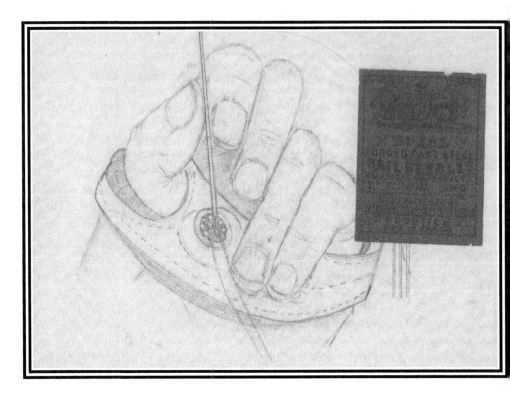

Palm and Needle

AN AUSSIE STOWAWAY
1968

I being my story ,by saying I played a part in this man's fate. Right or wrong.
Politicians, send young men in to war, but they themselves would hide in their cellar
or behind some excuse as many have, to avoid going with the great chance of not
returning.
It is those so call generals and politicians that stand by the Memorials with their rows
of medals and have not stood upon a battlefield under fire.
 War ,there is no glory or victors,Just men left with ghosts that never leave them
All we can do is remember. They say since WW2 the world is at peace,what
nonsense.
But its not...look at the world today its nothing but war and conflicts and
displacement of millions who suffer in poverty and homelessness because politicians
and the arms dealers continued selling armaments weapons of pointless destruction
and death. And we have lost the real sense of all those lost life's They would be
ashamed of us to see what we have made of their sacrifices.

I was at the time responsible for the general maintenance of the port side lifeboats. That entailed restocking fresh water in tanks,checking out of date foods such as biscuit, barley sugar and tinned milk (Connie Onnie)They may have been out of date but the barley sugar was still edible.

Painting the interiors of lifeboats and sanding oars and masts kept me busy throughout the voyage to Australia and New Zealand.

Our passenger were £10 migrates, making a new life.

It was the return voyage after departing from Freemantle,, the third day at sea I went to step in number 8 lifeboat and found a young Aussie in the bilge between the thawths,

I asked him,,thinking at first he was a passenger. "What are you doing, passengers are not allowed in lifeboats?"

But instead he said "Guess you could call me a stowaway!

"And how long have you been hiding?"

"Came on board in Freemantle mate!"

"So what have you been eating since?"

 Been eating what people leave and half drunk beer and water from your tank here"

He looked unkept in his appearance but healthy.

"So why this ship matie ,you know we are going back to England?"

 "Yes ,I know just had to get out of Aussie,mate or I would be on a plane going to Vietnam to fight in a war we have no right doing"

I had read somewhere many Australian had their birth dates are pulled out of the hat,much like a lottery.

At the time my stance on that war was as many Americas who protested the war in Vietnam. It was politicians and President war, the lies they told the American people to justify the continuous fighting a losing war and the death rate was getting higher.

 I didn't report him ,instead I gave him food ,beer and a change of clothes, and rigged up a tarpaulin against rain and sun.

Our next port of call ,was Durban South Africa. He even went ashore to the Seamen Mission,to write postcards home to his family being the only son, and his girlfriend.

The homeward voyage, took us close to the |Island of Tristan du Cunha, the most remote inhabited archipelago,along Gough Island,an inaccessible Wildlife Reserve,back inOctober1961,the volcano called Queen Mary's Peak,erupted and the population of some 250 souls were evacuated,and taken to the UK.

Many of the younger men worked on the Union Castle Royal Mail ship,others settle over in Fawley across the water from Southampton.

Sometime later the older one returned to the Island.

Madeira ,was our last port of call, Danny was so looking forward stepping ashore in Southampton and escaping the Vietnam war, where the new reported high number of young soldiers killed just young lads eighteen ,nineteen years old.

Then it happened...

Just after picking up the ships pilot at Nab Tower, one of my own department shopped him to the ships Master at Arms who took Danny into custody until we

docked, Then handed over to the police. He was later deported back to Aussie.
 The following voyage we arrived in Freemantle, I was working, when someone said there was someone at the gangway wishing to see me.
When I got there it was Danny. The remains of a black eye still showed plus he said a few other bruise under his tee shirt .Beaten and discharged
We went for a beer and he thank me for my support.
I knew I was right in helping that eighteen year old lad especially when he told me fifteen of his friends had been killed within three day after being sent to Vietnam. We kept in touch for a while until he moved to Cairns,Queensland My last correspondence was he had pasted his exams to become a lawyer,

BYE BYE CHIEF

Due to the times and awareness that ship could be a target for terrorists pirates and hijackers,some shipping companies took steps to protect its passengers and crews. Too make it more realistic we had a job creating a number of fake bombs,which we CPO Coxswain's had fun doing.

First was to find any old broken clocks or wrist watches to act as timers,then some thing to be used as explosives,which we decided broom handles sawn in to eight inch lengths,some electric wiring and tape to create our fake bombs.

The broom handle lengths were painted red to represent dynamite four to six to a bundle, clock, wiring and then taped.

The morning of the excise we hid six all over the ship giving the bridge their locations. When the alarm bell rang for the bomb drill,each crew member was responsible for searching their own cabins,then each department had their own areas to search which included work areas locker cupboards ,store rooms bars paint locker etc.

On the bridge each Officer did a quick search of their own cabin The watch coxswain was responsible for searching the Commodore or Captain's quarters. Which one needed the keys to ensure all lockers were searched in the Captain's cabin which included the drinks cabinet. To which once I ,myself was on the bridge and was given the keys to which the Commodore said " The bottles have be marked so crafty nips?" followed by a grin.

The crew if no bomb was found would report to their supervisor who would report to the bridge ,but if it was known to the bridge to be a part of the ship a bomb had been hidden it was made to search again.

On completion of the drill any fake bombs that had not been found were collected. As I mentioned at the start of the drill first thing each crew member searched their own quarters and sometime its where we hid them. So proving some were not taking it serious or had not even bothered.

Now we C.P.O's liked to have a laugh. So we had made a extra fake bomb, and after the drill we hid one in the bowl of his toilet in his cabin then cling filmed the bowl and dropped the lid and left.

It was the following morning when we mustered The Chief sat in his office and the expression on his tanned face told us he had discovered our little present,and the note which laid on his desk BYE BYE CHI EF. Like Queen Victoria ,he wasn't amused. But we had to grin at the thought of him lifting the lid.

Then he smiled and told us to sling our hooks and get to work.

Then sometime later we were moored alongside in San Pedro, Los Angeles. And the alarm's went off thinking a first it was a fire .So Fire teams got kitted up in our fire gear and waited to find out the location. The the Captain said they had received a bomb scare.

Meanwhile the US Fire department arrived and two firemen were allocated to each team. To help with the search.

Our two firemen helped search places like to forward stores and paint locker and one fireman made a comment "Christ this is a nightmare where does one start to search Anyone planting a bomb on a ship with a thousand hiding places it could be anyway even in one of these fifty drums of paint".

After a couple of hours searching it was found to be a fake caller..

But, what did come to the surface consequently that evening was most of the crew were ashore and there was not enough crew to cover the emergence to search. It was later decided to create 'In Port Manning' That meant a certain number of crew member from each department,how ever small had to stay on board while in port to cover in case of any further fire or bomb scares occurring in the future.

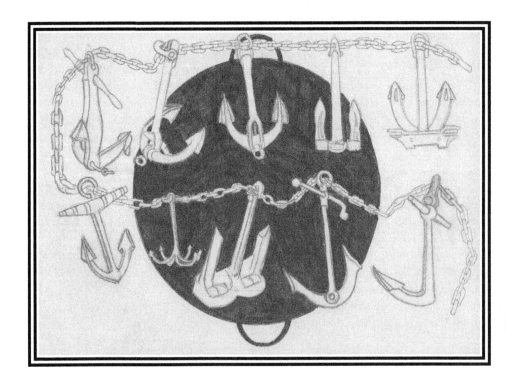

Old Shanghai

GNOME DOES A WORLD CRUISE

YES!! sounds strange a garden gnome doing a world cruise
Colin,was a mate of mine, he had not long been discharged from the Army.
He had a colourful career first in the Guards,then some time in the SAS seeing action
in a number of places.
But he had collection of garden gnomes scattered around his garden. Something one
wouldn't thing someone like him would have. But each their own right?"
One evening he invited me to a BBQ with friends and family at his place,
his collection was more than I expected everywhere one looked there was a gnome
peering over a wall behind bushes and in the thick vegetation of his back garden ,even
a few in the trees looking like snipers. But fun.
That evening I left late and nicked one.
It would be a week before I was due to return to my ship that was shorty to sailed on
a world cruise for a few month.
First it was to New York, then to Fort Lauderdale Florida, then off around the world.
To which I had voyaged many time over the years at sea on a variety of ships. But the
QE2 was a fine liner and I had done a number of world cruise aboard her. Working on
deck..

The idea was to take our gnome along and being a dab hand with a paint brush was
to paint it in costume of each place we visited. Which I did first the gnome was
painted as a hippie from San Francisco, then a Hawaiian in Honolulu and changed to
a Tahitian on our visit to Bora Bora in grass skirt and leis of flowers around its neck.
In New Zealand painted as a Maori,in Aussie change to a Aboriginal native.
Each time a photograph was taken. From Port Moresby Papua New Guinea,Japan,
China, Korea, Thailand each country our roaming gnome was repainted,even as a
Captain in his dinner uniform with black tie.
.
Now I must add those photographs would be prove ,but on leave I had been renting a
old WW2 Air Sea RAF Rescue launch, which had been converted in to a house boat.
When one early morning during the dead of winter and the river frozen .a small cat
wild cat that had found its self a home and had become part of the fixture woke me
with her meows to which when I opened the door there was a flash over the whole
boat was ablaze. To which at first I was trapped in the aft cabin and bedroom .
Which was once the Engine room and the false panelling bulkhead was covering the
once two large holes for the exhausts so I had to move the bed and break though to
exit the boat , feet first I went out thinking it was going to be cold and freezing went
hitting the water but it was frozen and I was wearing only a jumper underpants and no
shoes. The fire brigade had problems reaching me and the blazing boat as it was some
way from the road.
When finally the fire was extinguished and cause investigated it was found to be
wiring between the galley anf lounge bulkhead. The Fire Chief, asked me.What time I

had turned in and did I smell the electrics smouldering?

Which I didn't. But he had said using the old exhaust was very clever and had saved my life. As for the little kitten she was the hero if it hadn't been for her meowing and living on the boat. I may not be here. But she lost her life saving mine .

I lost everything among things were all the photographs of that garden gnome.

Colin's gnome was returned but a little changed in dress when he saw the gnome he asked his wife had she bought him another gnome ,to which she had no idea or had bought him another

But there it was, a grin on its face wearing a garland of bright tropical flowers around his neck.

There is a believe when humans retire to bed and the moon is full and high gnomes are said to come alive . So that night that well voyaged gnome had lot of adventures to tell his fellow gnome..

"See to the boy Surgeon"

"HERE YOU DUMP IT"
1971

Some older semen may remember when many Red Duster flagged ship had not just crews but a menagerie of animals. A dog ,cat ,parrot even a monkey or something more exotic that roamed around the alleys and decks. And stories passed down on who or how they came to be aboard.

Now in Savannah Georgia,the warehouses were full of feral cats that roamed and lived among the cargoes and store that fill those warehouses.

One day while walking through the shed I saw a cute, one colouration was that of grey white with a fleck of brown and two eye patches with the greenish eyes.

Stooping down I tempted it to come towards me but was no t forth coming. So left and went in to town .passing a small pet shop bought some treats .

Upon my return I saw the same young cat and again stopped and placed a little treat on the stone floor. And stepped back to watch the kitten approach the treat and sniff then eat the treat. Then I place another and another then turned away but my new little furry friend had taken the bait and followed me at distance. At the bottom of the gangway I turned to see it sat in the doorway of the shed in anticipate that I had more treats so I sat and waited then it came towards me slowly until it was almost by my feet then slowly walked up to me brushing against my leg. I was able to pick it up and was surprised it let me so I took it on board to my cabin and placed it on my bunk and gave it a few more treats.

Then watched as it played with the cord of a sweatshirt biting and rolling around on my blanket. Seem be making itself at home.

That first night it got on the bunk and made itself comfortable at the foot of the bunk. Then as weeks turned to months he was comfortable around the other lads.

I hadn't given it a name.

It was just "Cat"

During rounds I would take it to the fore peak out of the way.

It turned into a fine looking cat.

Then one morning during smoko there was a knock on the cabin door and in walked the Chief Master at Arms.. who said "I am lead to believe you have a cat right?"

"I do ?"I replied .

"So I believe?"

"And if did what about it?"

He straighten up pulled back his shoulders like he was back in the Royal Marines And said "Get rid of it?"

To which I asked "How should one get rid, as you put it Chief?"

!"Just put it a sack and dump it over the side?"

I just looked at the ginger haired brute,turned pick up the cat and popped it into a paper bag and handed it to him saying "Here you dump it".

He stepped back refusing to take the bag and its contents . The look on the Bootneck's face was priceless.

For a moment he just stood as if he was frozen holding the paper bag then push it towards me "Not my damn cat sailor?"
I wouldn't even consider doing such a thing to such a helpless cat.
On the other hand nothing would have stopped me if the boot was on the other foot and he was in need of rescuing it would be so easy to turn my back and walk away.

I heard one of the older long serving stewardess was retiring at the end of the voyage So asked her would she love a beautiful well trained cat. I invited to come see it.
She fell in love with it straight away and so that little kitten I picked up in Savannah,found itself a nice new cosy home to grow old and be loved.

Some months later the same Master at Arms crossed my path one and ask "What of the cat?"
"Oh didn't you know Chief,it got tossed over the side mid Atlantic as you ordered me it may have made land who knowns?"
That bull necked ex boot-neck, stood as if shock that I carried out he request.
I could see in his face the shock. But I was enjoying the guilt of asking me to do such a act.
But I told him what had happened really to the cat, He looked relieved and carried on his way down the working alleyway turning only to look back at me smiling.

NEW YORKS FINEST

A short story of a friend who had a change of careers.
He once worked on the Queen of Bermuda in the Catering Department he was also a
good musician and with a few mate on board they would entertain the crew.
His surname was Goodman so got the the nickname 'Benny' Goodman,after the well
know musician from WW2.
Now Benny got married to a New York women and settled down and became a New
York policeman.

So when in the Big Apple, we would catch up with each other whenever possible.
Sometimes he would drive down and park under the overpass near the ship and we
would sit in the car catching up and sharing a bottle of Southern Comfort. Other times
he was on duty by made a effort to drop by with his partner Dennis,an African
American, really a nice guy.
During the period when the Black Panther movement were active they both wore
those button badges that were very popular back then.
Dennis had on a black panther riding a white pig and Benny had one of a white pig

riding a black panther, What sense of humour between best friends and partners.
 Took a ride one day up to Skid Row in the city, what a eye opener. They parked up and we observed the entertaining going on.
 Nearby at a set of traffic light, a guy with bucker and squeezie steps out and starts to wash a guys car window,but the driver can be seen waving away the man washing his windows, then being asked for a gratuity but being refuse .as another man smashes a bottle in a paper bag against the front bumper then kick glass against the cars tryer so stopping the man from driving away and is forced to give a tip before the broken bottle is removed.
 Asking my policemen friends "Surely that wrong?"
Benny turned to me in the back seat,"Waste of time Terry, arrested them they barely have enough money to eat and there are important villains out there?"
 Then Dennis said ,"How many women do you see out there? Ten twenty? all profession street walking many are druggies,
It was certainly a eye opener.

   Another time we met up they were both off duty so we went to a diner,
I have always noticed with Americans how they leave their change on the counter.
This day we Dennis ,Benny and I,were sat eat and I notice a very dubious character come in the door of the diner. And came and sat on the seat next to mine. Without being to obvious I noticed he looked at my change laying on the counter.
When Dennis,said "The apple pie here is just like my mum's you should try it?"
for a moment I took my eye off the guy next to me.
But Benny didn't,then I felt someone's arm across my mid drift,looking down it was Benny's and in his hand he held a snubbed nose revolver. Followed my his badge.
And in a quiet low voice said to the stranger" Leave the coinage friend,and leave, its your lucky day,your excused as it a rather barmy day and I'm in a good mood, So disappear?"
I look at the man who I guess wasn't expecting that. He stood picked up his bag and before leaving grabbed a handful of salted crackers that were on the counter and scurried out.
 At the time there was some big Houhora . The press were reporting on a case where city officials and cops had been charged with corruption. It was1972 a police officer under cover called Frank Serpico had uncovered them.
But the corruption went high and Serpico was walking a dangerous line. He was later set up on a raid he entered first and got shot no one was ever convicted for attempted murder of Officer Serpico.
He was awarded the Medal of Honour,by the then Mayor Lindsey, but in a private and closed door ceremony.
Benny and Dennis knew Frank very well, saying he was one of New Yorks finest. It was said after Frank's hospitalisation, he went to live somewhere in Europe.

IN THE FOOTSTEPS OF ROERT LOUIS STEVENSON

We all have a favourite author that we read for many reasons.
Mine became a writer that was born in a different century and suffered most of his life
with ill health,but was a household name for his writing and adventures as a traveller
seafarer. In his later year was most respected among the inhabitants of Western
Samoa to which even in the twentieth century is still very revered among the islanders
as 'Tusitala', the Story Teller.

I became a collector of his works over the decades and before every voyage I would
pack in my bag a few copies of his works.

It all started as a young boy picking up a copy of 'The Ship's Cook'. Shame, I don't
still have that as it would be rare. It is better know as 'Treasure Island'.
As a young man ,when on leave after a voyage having no home to return to ,I would
go north to the Highlands of Scotland and just hike through the hills and glens like
Allen Beck of Stevenson's 'Kidnapped' sleeping under the stars and hearing the faint
distant lone swirl of the bagpipes drifting on the wind like a long forgotten ghost of
some distant clan.
Forgive the romantic, but a land of glen and mountains, lochs and heather, brings
forth the imagination when totally alone sat on a high ridge or taking shelter in a
crumbled stone crofters cottage.
An account titled 'Across the Plains' was a journey taken by RLS, from east to west
by stage coach fending off hostile Indians and other peoples.
In Montaray California there stand a building that was once the home of the

Stevenson's which is a museum today and open to all. It was somewhere I always wanted to visit and so I went on arrival it was closed ,but I sat under a gnarled old tree where Stevenson may have sat writing. How long I sat there in shade of that tree from the hot baking sun, time flew,when a woman unlocked the door,inviting me in. The only visitor.

We spoke long, In one room where he had written the Ships Cook (later renamed and printed as Treasure Island) was his jacket on the back of the chair. My host allowed me to sit at his desk looking out through the very same window where he had,with pen in hand.

The female curator before my departure said she had ben working in the house seven years and had never known anyone who had come through the door with so much knowledge and so versed in the authors life .and even offered me a job,which I explained it was not possible. But told her my voyage would be taking me to the island of Apia soon to visit his resting place.

Stevenson had voyaged across the Pacific visiting the Islands of Hawaii,became good friends with the Hawaiian Princess Kaiulani until her death. At the young age of just twenty three.

He also spent time in Sydney Australia.

Over the years and the numerous time I went to Pago Pago U.S Samoan Islands. I never got across to Apia.

 Samoa,is a beautiful place Island ans a spiritual and cultural heart of Polynesia. Its people are warm and friendly and most welcoming.

Back in the early year when we sailed in to the bay above us was a cable car and upon arrival the cable car would drop thousands of petals of tropical flowers that would fall and flutter down on the decks of the ship as a Samoan Aloha.

Some one I had acquainted was Michael ,a Samoan ships pilot. This one time he was our pilot and after we had dock met up.

I asked him about the easiest way to visit Apia.

He asked me, "Why do you wish to visit?"

"I have always wanted to visit the resting place of Tusitala,atop of Mount Vaea and walk the 1,148ft "Road of the Loving Heart".

He gave me the largest Samoan hug and said "It would be his honour to take me.

So it was agreed on the date to which I would be back would be on my birthday 10th March.

And on that day he was waiting I was off duty and we drove to the airport and flew in a light aircraft to the island. Some time prior Bonnie,a dearest friend had visited Vailima and sent me photos of herself standing on the terrace of Stevenson's home. Now I have finally made it.

When Stevenson,first arrived the different tribes were warring tribes, to which he couldn't accept and brought about peace between them all and never again raised the spear

When he died all the Chiefs,came together for their Tusitala,and it were they only that hacked their way through the thick vegetation to the summit of Mount Vaea.

Then carried him to his resting place.
A simple stone plinth with a stone casket, engrave with these words
"Here he lies where he longs to be "Home is the Sailor,Home from the Sea,And the Hunter Home from the Hill"
I could not have asked for no better birthday gift.
Finally arriving in San Francisco,I went to find a monument erected in his memory.

Some of my collection.. R.LStevenson. An Inland Voyage,Travels with a Donkey, Virginibus Puerisque,Treasure Island, Black Arrow,Memories&Portraits, The Child's Garden Verse, Prince Otto,The Merry Men, Underwood,Father Damien,A Open Letter,Island Nights Entrainment,Across the Plains, Moral Emblems,The Beach at Falesa,Catriona, Kidnapped,South Seas,Ebb Tide, Ballads,The Silverado Squatters,Letter to Family&Friends,Lay Moral Etc,Wrong Box,The Dynamiter,New Arabian Nights,A Christmas Sermon,Prayers Written in Vailima, Talk and Talkers,Songs of Travels, Edinburgh Picturesque Notes,A Mature Migrant,Will of the Mill, A Footnote to History,Dr Jekyl and Mr Hyde,A Note of Realism,The Wreckers, Memories of Fleming Jenkins,Records of a Family Engineer,Tales and Fantasies. St Ives and Weir of Hermiston unfinished. RLS 1878-1902

Cape Hinchbrook Lighthouse
Lat N60 11 07   lonW116 32 29

Lawyer Island Malacca Passage
Lat N 54 05 50   LonW130 19 86

Katie Rests

A FEW FRIENDS

Voyaging, is not just water weather and work it about friend whether they be fellow crew members or those people who's paths one may cross when ashore or those serendipity chance meetings. Some times one doesn't understand the language,other times you do.

Sometimes one is invited to share a meal or just sit a converse and pass a few hours in good company.

Such as Chester, A quiet kind of person well weathered face had lived life and see much and had a few ghosts. He was a fighter pilot during the Vietnam war and now lived in a small log cabin he built up a secluded inlet in Skagway Alaska,.and had a one winged bald eagle as a companion he had rescued during the Exon Valdez,oil spill in Alaska. The eagle had swooped to catch a salmon and its wing got coated in cruel oil and in the attempt to take flight beat it wings so hard it shattered its bones in its left wing so had to be amputated hence becoming flightless it was resigned to sit on Chester balcony railing as a guardian..and called Prince Willi

Chester, was a seaplane pilot buzzing all over Alaska ferrying workers and tourist to destination.

I was in Ketchikan one day waiting on the pontoon he was due in shortly. Dougie, in the office had been in radio contact say there were strong cross winds in the channel, Some moments later I heard the planes engine and watched as he came in to view Wings dipping and veering due to the strong Chinnock wind. Then as his floats almost touch the water the winds flipped the plane and came to rest upside down,to which a boat raced out as Chester fell out the cockpit of the plane uninjured,waving all was okay

He was brought in safely while another boat went to tow the plane to the pontoon.
"Glad to see your okay Chester " As we shook hands and walked in to the office.
"Nasty that wind today?" said Doug, as he pour Chester four fingers of Jack Daniels.
Then another.

Meanwhile, four young Americans sat with their backpacks awaiting their flight. All
open mouthed and in disbelief at what had just taken place... and how calm the pilot
was.

We spoke briefly he told me he would be in Skagway and would be home three days
and would pick me up once arriving in Skagway.

Dougie gave his new flight plans,He grabbed his gear turned said goodbye and open
the door,then turned again saying to the four guys "Well are you coming haven't got
all day?"

They couldn't believe they were his next bunch of passengers. A replacement plane
was already along side the pontoon waiting..

We did meet up and Prince William the bald eagle greeted me as I walked up the
ramp to Chester's cabin holding a bottle of Laphroaig Malt whiskey as a gift.

He wanted to show me his latest project he had built a run up to a natural lake so
salmon could run and lay their eggs. They had been spawning well.

There was Jack again another ex Vietnam Vet lived on an island off Costa Rica,
flew gunship choppers . He was shot down twice. He opened up once, told me he kept
having flash backs,his young gunner just nineteen,one moment in the chopper gun
firing, then next second a rocket explode in the cabin and Jack was covered in his
gunners blood and parts as he tried to fought to keep te chopper airborne. It had
haunted him for years.

But on the island he was just one of a few people that had found themselves a
sanctuary Trying to keep the ghosts at bay

I liked the evenings when they would have their BBQ Jack was the the cook, and
made burgers from crab lobster and prawn and were very tasty.

He just love the songs of singer Jimmy Buffet singing along as he threw those burgers
in the aid twisting around and catching the burger on a bun . He also loved his
Bombay gin, drank it like water. but no nicer guy would one want to call friend.

Gino an Hawaiian, who I met when he worked for Jardine a shipping agent out of
Honolulu,he would stay on board as we cruised the islands. He had spent some time at
sea. He retired later to settle down on the Big Island, and build a home and got few
animals. His wife Yolanda,was in the Air Force and they came to England all the way
from Hawaii for nothing just catching military flight because she had a pass that
allowed her to do so. It was good to see them and stayed with us at Longleat, when
my wife and I worked for the then Lord Bath, as his cook housekeeper and I was his
chauffeur. We met again, we live here in France they flew in for a Mediterranean
cruise with their grown children. A good dear friend who now has an degenerate eye
condition,but still a man with a great positive outlook.

When I was younger man I arrived in Moorea an island between Bora Bora and Tahiti. In my time off I went ashore to explore and by chance met a Tahitian same age,he was having a problem with his scooter so stopped to help,between us got it going a friendship that was to last forty eight years.

Each time and over the years that was many time I dropped anchor in Cooks Bay,Moorea. We would meet up Tua,with his family They were always waiting on the jetty,holding leis of flowers and shell necklaces as each member greeted me placing a lei over my neck. And each time I sailed away they would present me with a basket made of palm leave which contained assorted fish,fruits even breadfruits.

Tua, name translated means "wide ocean' or 'far distant'.,

During one visit the grandfather had disappeared,none of the family had any idea where he had gone . It was later found out he had won a national lottery and taken off visiting all his lost kin and relatives across the islands of the Pacific.

There are many, who I could mention good friends made while voyaging the world Throughout time and century,many have found themselves upon the oceans and seas,some not of their own choosing. In former times through being press ganged. In modern times some stay and becomes their life,others stay but a short time For myself it was my life ,I did try to go ashore once for a short time but when one hears the call of the sea I had to return Shore life was not for me, salt ran through my veins.

Someone once asked me "Don't you miss a normal life?
My reply was" I had a normal life, voyaged to every point of the compass card. Full of adventure,in good company. Certainly an education and amazing memories. And spent at sea in fresh clean sea air and winds in my face. And not a single days regret."

"Sure beats being woken by an alarm clock,rushing to work or to stand for an hour or two on a train you paid a high price for no seat,or drive to work in rush hour and heavy traffic,finding a parking space,get to work all stressed out,same desk,same view out the window for fifty years to get a handshake and presented with a clock.
Some hear the call of the sea ,others hear the cries of a child.

Through the Eyes of a Seafarer

List of Illustrations

Printed in Great Britain
by Amazon